מסורה

ArtScroll Mesorah Series®

Rabbi Nosson Scherman / Rabbi Meir Zlotowitz
General Editors

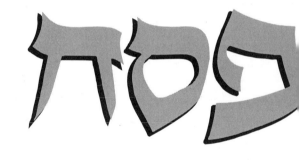

Insights by
Rabbi Shimon Finkelman
Laws by
Rabbi Moshe Dov Stein
and Rabbi Moshe Lieber
Overview by
Rabbi Nosson Scherman

pesach

PASSOVER — ITS OBSERVANCE, LAWS AND
SIGNIFICANCE / A PRESENTATION BASED ON
TALMUDIC AND TRADITIONAL SOURCES

Published by

Mesorah Publications, ltd

FIRST EDITION
First Impression . . . February 1994
SECOND EDITION
First Impression . . . February 1995
Second Impression . . . January 1998

Published and Distributed by
MESORAH PUBLICATIONS, Ltd.
4401 Second Avenue
Brooklyn, New York 11232

Distributed in Europe by
J. LEHMANN HEBREW BOOKSELLERS
20 Cambridge Terrace
Gateshead, Tyne and Wear
England NE8 1RP

Distributed in Israel by
SIFRIATI / A. GITLER—BOOKS
10 Hashomer Street
Bnei Brak 51361

Distributed in Australia & New Zealand by
GOLDS BOOK & GIFT CO.
36 William Street
Balaclava 3183, Vic., Australia

Distributed in South Africa by
KOLLEL BOOKSHOP
Shop 8A Norwood Hypermarket
Norwood 2196, Johannesburg, South Africa

ARTSCROLL MESORAH SERIES®
"PESACH" / Its Observance, Laws, and Significance

ISBN
0-89906-447-7 (hard cover)
0-89906-446-9 (paperback)

Typography by Compuscribe at ArtScroll Studios, Ltd.

Printed in the United States of America by Noble Book Press
Bound by Sefercraft, Quality Bookbinders, Ltd. Brooklyn, N.Y.

This book is dedicated
to the memory of

החבר אפרים בן הרב רפאל ז"ל
Edward F. Gugenheim

נפטר א' דר"ח תמוז תש"כב

A descendant of Rabbi Samson Rafael Hirsch,
he lived and breathed the noblest traditions
of German Orthodoxy.

He knew flight, danger, and struggle,
but never compromise.
His beliefs and allegiance
to the Torah never wavered.

He wanted one reward and it is richly his:
that his offspring and theirs
follow proudly and firmly in his footsteps.

ת. נ. צ. ב. ה.

Mrs. Etta Gugenheim and Family

Table of Contents

☙ Selected Laws and Customs

◆§ Publisher's Preface

To most of us, the word Pesach conjures up visions of the Seder and Haggadah. Indeed, more commentaries have been written on the Haggadah than on any other sacred work, and the ArtScroll Series, too, has published and continues to publish such works regularly.

But there is much more to Pesach, especially in the busy days and weeks leading up to it. This anthology concentrates on the "other" Pesach, apart from the Seder, on the festival's significance in Jewish life and the laws leading up to it, and contains a special section on the laws of that complex rarity in the Hebrew calendar, an Erev Pesach that falls on the Sabbath.

This book contain three sections:

— The **Overview**, like the others in the ArtScroll Series, presents a *hashkafah*/philosophical perspective on major concepts of the festival.

— The **Insights**, by the familiar and much-admired **Rabbi Shimon Finkelman,** presents a rich and fascinating collection of Rabbinic thought, anecdotes, homilies, and interpretation.

— The **Laws and Customs** offers a broad selection of the laws leading up to Pesach. There is also a thorough treatment of *Shabbos Erev Pesach*, including a chronological step-by-step checklist of pertinent details and a table of relevant times encompassing the next two occurrences of this event. The Laws Section has been compiled by **Rabbi Moshe Dov Stein,** *moreh hora'ah* of Kehillas Sh'or Yoshuv, Far Rockaway, N.Y., and our colleague **Rabbi Moshe Lieber.** It is adapted from Rabbi Stein's acclaimed Hebrew work, *Aliba D'Hilchasa*. We are grateful to the staff members who extended themselves to produce this work. Its every page testifies to their dedication. They are: Mrs. Judy Dick, Mrs. Mindy Stern, Mrs. Faygie Weinbaum, Mrs. Ethel Gottlieb, Yehuda Gordon, Mrs. Bas Siyon Drebin, Mrs. Bassie Gutman, Nichie Fendrich, Dvory Glatzer and Chaya Gitti Zaidman.

The trying task of paginating this book was done with grace and professionalism by Mrs. Mindy Breier. R' Eli Kroen's creative touch in designing such an attractive cover is another example of the beautification of Torah literature for which he constantly strives.

Rabbi Meir Zlotowitz/Rabbi Nosson Scherman
General Editors

Adar, 5754
February, 1994

ᴇ§ An Overview — Pesach: The Essence of Redemption

An Overview —
Pesach: The Essence of Redemption*

I: Seeds and Growth

From Potential to Reality

In explaining the transition from *Bereishis*/Genesis to *Shemos*/Exodus, *Ramban* describes how one book flows from the other. The Book of Genesis charts the development of the Patriarchs into a family, while the Book of Exodus shows how the seeds planted by the Patriarchs blossomed into the destiny of their offspring. Thus, Genesis and Exodus, respectively, record Israel's progression from זְרִיעָה to צְמִיחָה, from *planting* to *blossoming*.

Genesis and Exodus, respectively, record Israel's progression from planting to blossoming.

Genesis is the story of creation, not primarily the formation of the universe, but of the Patriarchal family that God charged with the responsibility to infuse the world with sanctity and purpose. After Ishmael and Esau were removed from the families of Abraham and Isaac, Jacob completed that aspect of history by forming a family that was completely righteous, freed from base and evil influences. Then, the seeds sown in Genesis had to grow and be nurtured. That would be the next stage.

The Book of Exodus continues the story. It tells how the family of seventy people grew into a nation of millions, how it survived and surmounted exile, experienced salvation through God's direct intervention, received the Torah, and, finally, built the Tabernacle, as the resting place on earth of the *Shechinah*, or God's Presence. Only then, when the *Shechinah* was among them, was the צְמִיחָה, *blossoming*, complete, for then, as *Ramban* puts it, the Jewish people had "returned to the heights of their forefathers." The Patriarchs and Matriarchs are described as the מֶרְכָּבָה, *chariot*, meaning that their very essence was to serve God; just as a chariot is an

Only then, when the Shechinah was among them was the blossoming complete.

---

* The Overview is based primarily on the thought of Rabbi Gedaliah Schorr in *Ohr Gedaliahu*.

extension of its rider, extending his presence and power to new areas, so the Patriarchs and the Matriarchs lived only to serve Him and bring His teachings to others, by word and example.

This concept of Genesis as planting and Exodus as blossoming is foreshadowed in the very beginning of the story of Creation. The Sages note that the word אוֹר, *light*, appears five times in the account of the first day, corresponding to the Five Books of Moses and alluding to the concept that the only true light is the Torah — the source of wisdom and holiness. The Torah's first two references to light are *let there be light* and *and* *The Book of there was light (Genesis* 1:3). The Book of Genesis *Genesis symboli-* symbolizes the command that man and his universe be *zes the command* *that man and his* illuminated, not only through the heavenly bodies, but *universe be illumi-* through the Book that tells how the Patriarchs and *nated, through the* *Patriarchs and* Matriarchs laid the groundwork — planted the seeds — *Matriarchs.* for the giving of the Torah and the birth of the nation that would accept it and personify it.

The Book of Exodus is the fulfillment of that command. In it, Israel becomes first a nation, and then *God's* nation, by accepting the Torah and building the Tabernacle that will house His glory on earth. As *Ramban* expressed it, Genesis is the seed and Exodus is its growth.

וְהָיָה מִסְפַּר בְּנֵי־יִשְׂרָאֵל כְּחוֹל הַיָּם אֲשֶׁר לֹא־יִמַּד וְלֹא יִסָּפֵר . . .

The count of the Children of Israel shall be like the sand of the sea, which cannot be measured and cannot be counted (Hosea 2:1).

Tran- The Talmud raises the difficulty that this verse seems to *scending* contradict itself. It begins by speaking of the *count* of *Limitations* Israel, implying that there *can* be an exact census, and it concludes by saying that Israel *cannot* be counted. The Talmud explains that the verse alludes to two different levels of Jewish accomplishment. When they do not serve God properly, they are finite and limited; when they do the will of God, there is no limit to their greatness; they *cannot be counted (Yoma* 22b).

Chiddushei HaRim offers a further insight into the verse's message. The prophet reveals that the Jewish people exists on two levels: On the one hand, we live in a physical world, where everything can be quantified and potential is limited by material constraints. A human being can lift only so many pounds and human intelligence can go only so far. But on a different level, Israel can aspire to a world where miracles are commonplace and where people can attain spiritual levels that are indeed infinite and cannot be quantified. Thus there is no contradiction in the words of Hosea: We are counted in terms of our physical limitations, and simultaneously we cannot be counted because our souls can soar above the obstacles of everyday life.

We are counted in terms of our physical limitations, and simultaneously we cannot be counted because our souls can soar above the obstacles of everyday life.

This explains one of the ten miracles that occurred regularly in the Temple. On Yom Kippur, there was such a crush of people that there was barely room enough for them to stand, but when the time came for them to confess their sins, they could prostrate themselves and beg forgiveness without anyone being close enough to hear their embarrassing admissions (*Avos* 5:7). Jews lived in a world of two dimensions, physical and spiritual. In terms of square feet, they were woefully overcrowded, but when their spiritual needs required them to have privacy, the physical world stood aside and made room for them.

Overriding Nature This dual nature of the Jewish people was foreshadowed at the beginning of our existence, at the time when God promised Abraham that he and Sarah would have an heir (see *Genesis* 15:1-6). As the Sages elaborate on the dialogue between God and Abraham, even after God promised Abraham that he would have a son, Abraham protested that his reading of the constellations showed that he was incapable of having a child. God responded that he should abandon his reliance on the science of astronomy and trust in God's promise, for the destiny of Israel transcends natural law (see *Rashi* there and *Shabbos* 156a-b). But this account raises difficult questions. How could Abraham, the man of perfect faith, question God's promise? How could he even imagine that his reading of the stars had

How could Abraham, the man of perfect faith, question God's promise?

greater validity than God's clear and unequivocal pledge?

In an insight of penetrating brilliance, *Chiddushei HaRim* explains that Abraham's question did not stem from insufficient faith. Rather, it was clear to him that God's promise had struck down the law of nature, just as the Splitting of the Sea at the time of the Exodus suspended the law of gravity, as the waters piled up into a huge wall until Israel had crossed to safety. Consequently, when Abraham looked at the constellations again after God's promise, he was sure that their message would have changed to reflect the new reality *He looked at the* that he and Sarah would have a son. He looked at the *stars to see how* stars not to see if God was right, but to see how the *the heavens bowed* heavens bowed to the word of their Master. But the *their Master. But* constellations had *not* changed! Nature still declared *the constellations* that he and Sarah would remain childless. Why had they not heeded God's word?

In response, God taught him an eternal principle of Israel's existence — then and forever. Nature had not changed. The stars still insisted that Abraham and Sarah were and would continue to be barren. But God's promise would be fulfilled in spite of nature; they would have a child anyway.

The constellations Yes, Abraham, God responded. The constellations *have not changed,* have not changed, but Israel's destiny transcends what *but Israel's destiny* nature claims to be incontrovertible. Abraham and *transcends nature.* Sarah *will* have a son — even though it is "impossible." Their offspring *will* emerge from Egyptian slavery purified and strengthened — even though it is impossible. They *will* survive destruction, exile, persecution, hunger, and holocaust — even though it is impossible. They would even be subject to an exact, finite count — and it will still be impossible to count them.

This was the message of Hosea, as set forth above. God's nation lives in a natural *physical* world, but also thrives in a higher, *spiritual* world. Nature would always conspire against Israel. By all the laws of history, the Jewish people should have disappeared centuries ago. As the Passover Haggadah declares, "In every generation they stand up against us to destroy us, but God rescues us from their hand." Was there ever a century when this was clearer than ours, when nations were bent upon Jewry's destruction, whether through action or apathy?

II: Names

The Tribal Ancestors

The Hebrew name of the Book of Exodus is *Shemos*, or *Names*. Indeed, the first chapters of the Book deal extensively with names: the names of Jacob's sons who descended to Egypt with him (1:1-4), the reason Moses was given his name (2:10), and Moses' desire to know by what Name God wanted to be announced to the Jewish people (3:13-14). As it is elaborated upon in Rabbinic literature, the names used in the Torah imply the Divinely ordained nature and mission of the person or thing being named. Thus, when *Tanchuma* at the beginning of Exodus comments about Jacob's sons that "their names were seemly and their deeds were seemly," he means that not only did their names indicate that they were destined for greatness, but that they lived up to their potential. That is no mean achievement, for all too often those "most likely to succeed" fail to do so.

The names used in the Torah imply the Divinely ordained nature and mission of the person or thing being named.

In this sense, *Midrash Shemos Rabbah* (1:5) comments that the eventual redemption from Egypt was implied in the names of the twelve tribes, meaning that Israel's future greatness was already contained within the spiritual essence expressed in those names, much as the giant oak of the future already exists in microcosm within the seed that produced it. And just as a seed decays before the plant grows, so Israel would suffer mightily in Egypt before it was ready for its eventual redemption. The future, however, still lay in the seeds of the past, as indicated in the names of Jacob's sons, for, as *Ramban* comments (see above), the Egyptian exile did not begin until the seeds of the future had been planted by the experiences recounted in Genesis.

Just as a seed decays before the plant grows, so Israel would suffer before it was ready for its eventual redemption.

For example, the name Reuben — containing the words רְאוּ בֵּן, *see [a] son* — alludes to God's declaration that רָאֹה רָאִיתִי אֶת־עֳנִי עַמִּי, *I have indeed seen the affliction of My people (Exodus 3:7).* Thus, Reuben came to Egypt bearing the truth that when his offspring had suffered enough, God would intervene. In a deeper sense, the greatness of Reuben and the rest of the Jewish people was that they retained their uniqueness as עַמִּי, *My people.* In spite of all the affliction and degradation they suffered in Egypt, they persisted in being God's people.

This is the essential import of the Sages' teaching that the Jews in Egypt kept their Hebrew names. This is true, of course, in the literal sense that they used names as a way of keeping their Jewish identity, and thereby avoiding total assimilation into Egyptian society. In addition, however, they also kept their "names" in the spiritual sense, for although they sinned in many ways, they did not lose their essential purity — and this is what made it possible for them to hear God's voice and declare their loyalty to Him at Mount Sinai, only seven weeks after leaving Egypt.

They also kept their "names" in the spiritual sense, for although they sinned in many ways, they did not lose their essential purity.

III: Stars

Deceptive Size

Rashi comments at the beginning of Exodus that the Children of Israel are likened to the stars, which God counts when they appear at night and again when they disappear in the morning. So, too, God counted the tribal ancestors in life by enumerating them in the Book of Genesis and counting them again before they died, by listing their names again at the beginning of the Book of Exodus. By doing so, God showed that every Jew is important to Him, and if so, we must act accordingly; each of us matters and the deeds of every Jew are needed to fulfill God's scheme.

God showed that every Jew is important to Him, and if so, we must act accordingly.

But isn't an individual person insignificant? The song goes "Twinkle, twinkle, little star," but only a young child thinks the stars are truly little. We know that our sun, with all its mass and energy, is but an average-size star, and that there are countless stars in the solar system that are infinitely larger. So, too, every Jew. We are like stars. We *seem* small and insignificant, but only God knows how much we matter and how much difference we make in His "solar system" of the human race. So, too, just as it can take many, many years for the light of a star to reach earth, the influence of a single Jew may not be felt for a long time. That of the Patriarchs and the tribal ancestors is still with us — and we may never know when our *own* deeds may influence others, nor will they, but our impact may well be considerable.

Just as it can take many, many years for the light of a star to reach earth, the influence of a single Jew may not be felt for a long time.

Without question, the exile in Egypt was a difficult one, and it was made even harder because our ancestors had no Torah to sustain them. *We* know that there was a revelation at Sinai. *We* know that the Torah is the soul of our people and that it is our comfort, inspiration, and standard of behavior. But what did our ancestors have in Egypt, before the Torah was given?

They had the knowledge that they were children of Abraham, Isaac, and Jacob; that they were members of tribes whose founders bore names that signified the seeds of the future, that they were as precious, important, and huge as stars, small though they may have seemed to their Egyptian oppressors or those of their brethren who had fallen by the wayside.

Exile Is Relative

Because fallen Jews there were. *Chiddushei HaRim* comments that there were three categories of Jews. There were the few great ones who never felt exiled wherever they were, because they had complete faith that God was everywhere and that every ordeal had a purpose.

The average Jew was different. He *was* in exile. He had begun to sin, to neglect circumcision, to fall toward the forty-ninth level of spiritual contamination. But because he knew that his destiny should have been higher than that imposed by his Egyptian overseer, he maintained his name and language, and thereby remained a Jew even in Egypt. These were the simple Jews who rallied to Moses and Aaron, their ingrained faith revivified.

These were the simple Jews who rallied to Moses and Aaron, their ingrained faith revivified.

But, lamentably, there were other Jews who were not in exile — because they had become so thoroughly assimilated into Egyptian culture that they no longer felt like outsiders. They were not even fazed by being a despised and downtrodden underclass of slaves. In their eyes they had found a home in the land of their captivity and could not contemplate leaving it. Didn't many Jews complain in the Wilderness that they missed the delicious food they had received in Egypt *free of charge?* Forgotten was the backbreaking task of building the pyramids, the agony of having their infants thrown into the Nile or cemented into the walls — the food was *free* and everything they had to endure was part of life, something to be accepted.

Didn't many Jews complain in the Wilderness that they missed the delicious food they had received in Egypt free of charge?

Secure Borders

People are that way. They can learn to adjust to almost anything and accept it as a "normal" part of the human condition. The Sages teach that a slave could not escape from Egypt, to which the *Rebbe* of Izhbitza offers a novel but telling interpretation. Egypt was such a rich country that everyone considered himself fortunate to be there, an attitude that was fostered by the "propaganda" of the day. So powerful was this public perception that even slaves felt allegiance to the country — so much so that they could not bring themselves to escape; even without guards at the borders, they preferred to remain.

So powerful was this public perception that even slaves felt allegiance to the country.

How familiar all this sounds. Many Jews in every era are no less convinced that wherever they live is a paradise, that they have no need to change and that any talk of higher and nobler aspirations is seditious prattle that will rob them and their children of opportunity.

To counter such watchtowers and guard dogs of the spirit, Pesach comes every year.

To counter such watchtowers and guard dogs of the spirit, Pesach comes every year and reminds us that our ancestors were once in Egypt, the greatest and richest civilization of its era, where it would have been supremely easy for them to forget their origins — but they didn't. They tried to remember that they had within themselves the seeds of their forebears. They found ways to maintain their memories of their origins and their responsibility to remain unique and different.

Liberated Speech

The literature of Kabbalah teaches that during the depth of the Egyptian experience, the Jewish mouth — the power of self-expression — was in exile. Speech is man's great gift because it allows him to put his ideas and yearnings into words, to express himself in ways that others can comprehend. But in Egypt, Israel's speech was stifled and they were forced to accept mutely whatever Egyptian culture dictated. Then, with the redemption, the nation that wondered whether its roots still suckled from the wellsprings of the Patriarchs saw the hand of God, and when the Sea of Reeds split for them and swamped the Egyptians, they burst forth in praise, saying, זֶה אֵלִי וְאַנְוֵהוּ אֱלֹהֵי אָבִי וַאֲרֹמְמֶנְהוּ , *This is my God and I will build Him a Sanctuary; the God of my father and I will exalt Him (Exodus 15:2)*. Their power of speech exploded in a freedom they utilized to let the seeds within them flourish luxuriantly.

Because they did, we are here.

There are all sorts of exiles. There are those of drudgery and slavery, and there are those of comfort and abundance. Pesach reminds us that whichever it is, the "names" of our ancestors are part of us and we *can* let them come to the fore.

This is the true essence of our Festival of Freedom.

Rabbi Nosson Scherman
Shevat 5754/January 1994

➲ Insights

Crown of All Festivals
The Chametz Prohibitions
Erev Pesach
The Pesach Sacrifice
The Seder Night
Recounting the Details of the Exodus
The Four Cups
Matzah
Maror
Afikoman
Hallel
Counting the Omer
Chol HaMoed
The Seventh Day of Pesach
Song of Songs
Pesach Stories

Crown of All Festivals

בְּרֹאשׁ כָּל מוֹעֲדוֹת נִשֵּׂאתָ פֶּסַח.
Above all Festivals You elevated Pesach.

(*Passover Haggadah*)

A Moment in History

◄§ The festival of Pesach celebrates the central event of Jewish history, the redemption of the Jewish people from Egypt. The significance of this event is best evidenced by the fact that the Ten Commandments begin with the declaration, *I am HASHEM, your God, Who delivered you from the land of Egypt* (*Exodus* 20:2). The very fact that God introduces Himself as Redeemer rather than Creator serves to emphasize His unchanging role as Director of all that occurs on this earth. The miracles during the period of the Ten Plagues and the crossing of the Sea of Reeds demonstrated vividly how completely God controls every aspect of nature and bore testimony to His creation of every molecule of the universe.[1]

The giving of the Torah at Sinai was not only the result of the Exodus but, more important, the *purpose* of the Exodus. As God told Moses when He revealed Himself to him for the very first time: *'When you take the people out of Egypt, you will serve God on this mountain [i.e., Sinai]'* (*Exodus* 3:12). The Exodus was when the descendants of Jacob became God's Chosen Nation, but it was at Sinai that their nationhood was fully defined. In the words of *R' Saadiah Gaon, our nation is a nation only through Torah.*

The centrality of this Festival is evidenced by the number of *mitzvos* associated with it. *Rambam* enumerates three positive and five negative commandments relevant to Pesach, in addition to the four positive and twelve negative commandments relating to the *korban Pesach* (Pesach sacrifice), a total of twenty-four *mitzvos.*

In stark contrast to secular holidays, Jewish Festivals are far more than mere remembrances of events that happened long ago. Each

---

1. *Rabbeinu Yonah* offers another explanation for why the Ten Commandments begins with mention of the Exodus: God said to Israel, "My children, there are times when My commands may seem harsh and incomprehensible, but I ask you to trust that I mean it all for your benefit. Did I not redeem you from Egypt for your own sake? So, too, you may be certain that everything I ask you to do is not for My sake, but for yours."

Yom Tov (Festival) has its own unique spiritual light which reflects the day's essence. Pesach is זְמַן חֵרוּתֵנוּ, *the time of our freedom*. This refers not only to physical freedom, for the redemption from Egypt was far more than a release from physical bondage. Israel had been corrupted by the sinful environment of Egypt. It had fallen to the forty-ninth level of spiritual impurity [מ״ט שַׁעֲרֵי טוּמְאָה]. When God liberated the Jews, He lifted their souls from the baseness of falsehood and impurity to the loftiness of truth and purity. Each year on Pesach, the spiritual emanations that uplifted the Jews as they left Egypt flow from Above once more. It is for us to attune ourselves to the awesome sanctity of the holiday so that we might absorb its great light and liberate ourselves from our own spiritual failings.[1]

Two Names

◆§ The festival that we refer to as "Pesach" is referred to in the Torah and in the festival prayers as חַג הַמַצּוֹת, *the Festival of Matzos*. *Kedushas Levi* explains that these names reflect the love which God and His nation feel for one another. *Matzah* symbolizes the Jews' faith at the time of their redemption.

> *They baked the dough they took out of Egypt into cakes of matzah, for they could not be leavened, for they were driven from Egypt and could not delay, nor had they made provisions for themselves (Exodus 12:39).*
>
> This reveals how praiseworthy Israel was, that they did not say, "How can we go out into the Wilderness without provisions?" Rather, they had faith and departed. Thus does Scripture state *(Jeremiah 2:2): [So said Hashem:] 'I remember for your sake the kindness of your youth, the love of your bridal days, how you followed Me in the Wilderness in an unsown land' (Rashi ibid.).*

The name "Pesach" (which means *pass over*) alludes to the unique Providence with which God guides and protects His Chosen Nation:

---

1. The Torah refers to the month of Nissan in which the Exodus took place as חֹדֶשׁ הָאָבִיב, *the month of springtime (Exodus 13:4)*. This phrase is a key element in the Hebrew calendar because it ordains that Pesach always occur in springtime. Since twelve ordinary lunar months have only 354 days, a thirteenth month is added to the Hebrew calendar seven times every nineteen years in order that Pesach will indeed fall in the spring. The relationship between spring and the Exodus symbolizes the idea that the Jewish people always remain filled with the potential for spiritual renewal.

You shall say: 'It is a Pesach feast-offering to HASHEM, *Who passed over* [אֲשֶׁר פָּסַח] *the houses of the Children of Israel in Egypt when He smote the Egyptians, but He rescued our houses'* (*Exodus* 12:27).

In *Song of Songs*, the relationship between God and Israel is allegorically depicted as the relationship between a husband and wife.[1] Such a relationship must be predicated on mutual love, with each party recognizing the other's devotion toward him or her. The mutual love between God and Israel became revealed at the time of the Exodus. It is recognition of this love which is the very essence of the joy inherent in every *Yom Tov*. As we say in the prayers of each of the Scriptural Festivals: *You have chosen us from all the peoples; You loved us and found favor in us . . . And You gave us,* HASHEM, *our God, with love, appointed festivals for gladness, Festivals and times for joy. . . .*

Thus, the joy and essence of each of the Festivals are rooted in the Exodus. It is to this which the *Haggadah* alludes in stating: *Above all Festivals You elevated Pesach.*

The rigors of daily life can wear a person down and prevent a Jew from delighting in his being a part of the Chosen Nation for whom all of creation came into being. Each of the Festivals was granted us as a precious gift from Above, a time to rejoice in our lot and renew our closeness with God.

Free Forever

◆§ In the *Maariv* prayer recited year round, we praise God Who took us out of Egypt לְחֵרוּת עוֹלָם, *to eternal freedom*. From this term we see clearly that the redemption from Egypt was primarily a freedom of the spirit. In the words of the Lutzker *Rav*, R' Zalman Sorotzkin:

> Our main attainment in leaving Egypt was spiritual freedom from idolatry and the desire to follow God into a barren desert [where we received the Torah]. If we succeed in understanding this, then we will also understand how this freedom shall never again be erased, even during the physical subjugation of later exiles . . .
>
> . . . Had [the redemption of] the Children of Israel been delayed any more, they would have sunk to the fiftieth level

---

1. See p. 98

of spiritual impurity and become unredeemable. Compare the Jews of ancient Egypt to the Jews of today. In Egypt, the Jewish people did not possess the Torah, but still maintained their own language, culture, names, and manner of dress. Nevertheless, despite their adherence to these nationalistic traits which set them apart and the fact that they were in Egypt only two hundred and ten years, they could not survive as Jews even one moment more and would have become lost among the Egyptians. On the other hand, Jews have survived as a people in this exile for almost two thousand years. Protected by the Torah, we shall never become lost among the nations (*Oznayim L'Torah*).

Once, while traveling on a train, the *Alter* of Novorhadok (R' Yosef Yoizel Horowitz) found himself in the company of freethinkers. Taking note of the *Alter*'s rabbinic garb, they attempted to draw him into philosophical debate. The *Alter* told them, "You people call yourselves 'free,' for you have liberated yourselves from the restrictions of religious belief. In fact, you are slaves. I have disciplined myself to the extent that I am prepared to do whatever my Creator asks of me. You, on the other hand, are ruled by your passions and desires. *That* is real slavery."

Festival of Faith

◈§ As the time when God demonstrated His exacting Providence in this world, Pesach is also a festival most opportune for strengthening oneself in matters of *emunah*, Jewish faith. *Nesivos Shalom* puts it this way:

Pesach is חַג הָאֱמוּנָה, *the Festival of Faith,* and the *Seder* night, when the Divine Presence revealed itself [during the slaying of the firstborn[1], is רֹאשׁ הַשָּׁנָה לָאֱמוּנָה, *the New Year for Faith.* Through the clarity of faith of this night, one merits to live a life of faith throughout the year.

The central *mitzvah* of the *Seder* night is סִפּוּר יְצִיאַת מִצְרַיִם, *recounting the details of the Exodus from Egypt.* Relating the story of the Exodus is the primary means on this night of instilling faith in our children and in ourselves.

---

1. See p. 38

The Talmud (*Makkos* 24a) lists a number of great personalities in Scriptures who enumerated various ethical requirements as the basis for the fulfillment of all the Torah's commandments. "Habakuk came and established them [the commandments] upon one [ethical requirement], as it is written, *A righteous person lives by his faith*" (*Habakuk* 2:4).

There are many levels of *emunah*. The deeds of the righteous reflect a clarity of faith that is acquired through unstinting devotion to serving one's Creator. However, even the righteous can strive for yet greater heights in faith, for its levels of clarity are without limit.

Thus do we say on this night, "Even if we are all men of wisdom, understanding, experience and knowledge of the Torah, it would still be an obligation upon us to tell about the Exodus from Egypt. The more one tells about the Exodus from Egypt, the more he is praiseworthy."

Israel's Treasure

◄§ In his classic *Orchos Chaim*, *Rabbeinu Asher (Rosh)* writes:

> Trust in God with all your heart, and believe in His providence upon every detail. In this way, you will fulfill in your heart [belief] in His uniqueness, by believing that His eyes roam over the entire world, and are upon all the ways of men, testing their hearts and analyzing feelings. For whoever does not believe the phrase, *Who took you out of the land of Egypt* (*Exodus* 20:2), also does not believe [the preceding statement], *I am Hashem your God* — for such is not [proper belief] in His uniqueness. [Belief in His uniqueness] is Israel's treasure above all the nations and is the foundation of the entire Torah.

In the first of the Thirteen Principles of Faith (as formulated by *Rambam*), we declare our belief that God is the Creator of all and that He alone directs the happenings of His creations. In the second principle, we declare our faith in His uniqueness and add the phrase וְהוּא לְבַדּוֹ אֱלֹהֵינוּ, *and He alone is our God*. Through the Exodus, Israel became subject to a unique measure of *hashgachah pratis,* exacting Divine Providence, and thus stands apart in its belief in God's uniqueness. God's unity is affirmed not only by our belief in creation itself, but also by our belief in His being *our God,* Whose Providence is directed toward us in a very precise way *(Orach Yesharim).*

Lessons for Life

◆§ R' Eliyahu Lopian (author of *Lev Eliyahu*) once said that two comments of *Ramban* (Nachmanides) provide a Jew with a path for life. The first comment (*Exodus* 13:16) discusses the significance of the Exodus in Jewish belief. The following is drawn from that comment:

The great wonders and signs are faithful testimonies for belief in the Creator and in the entire Torah. The Holy One, Blessed is He, does not perform a wonder or sign in every generation; He therefore commanded us to forever make a remembrance and sign of that which our [ancestors'] eyes beheld. God was exceedingly stringent in this matter, as is evident from the punishment of *kareis* (spiritual excision) for [consumption of] *chametz* or for failing to offer the Pesach sacrifice. He commanded us to record that which we witnessed [in the *tefillin* which are worn] upon our arms and [upon our head] between our eyes; to inscribe it on the doorposts of houses on *mezuzos;* [1] to mention it with our lips every morning and evening, as it is written, *That you may remember the day when you came out of the land of Egypt, all the days of your life* (*Deuteronomy* 16:3); to construct a *succah* each year and perform many other *mitzvos* which are a remembrance of the Exodus from Egypt. All this is so that the wonders of the Exodus will never be forgotten and so that there will be no opportunity for a non-believer to preach denial of faith in God.

. . . And from the great and well-known miracles, one comes to recognize the hidden miracles, which are the foundation of the entire Torah. *For a man has no share in the Torah of Moses until he believes that all our happenings and*

---

1. The *mezuzah* contains the first two portions of the *Shema*, which contain no apparent references to the Exodus. It seems difficult to understand why *Ramban* lists *mezuzah* here.

The Brisker *Rav* offered two answers to this question. The two portions of *Shema* contained in the *mezuzah* both mention the *mitzvah* of *tefillin*, regarding which the Torah states: *and it shall be a sign upon your arm and an ornament between your eyes, for with a strong hand* HASHEM *removed us from Egypt* (*Exodus* 13:16; see full text of *Ramban* cited here).

Additionally, *Ramban*, in his commentary to the opening verse of the *Shema* (*Deuteronomy* 6:4), explains how that verse alludes to the wonders of the Exodus.

occurrences are miraculous — there is nothing natural in them at all.[1]

The second comment of *Ramban* to which R' Lopian referred is on the Torah's command: קְדֹשִׁים תִּהְיוּ, *You shall be holy (Leviticus* 19:2). In *Ramban's* memorable words, this means: קַדֵּשׁ עַצְמְךָ בְּמֻתָּר לָךְ, *sanctify yourself in that which is permitted to you.* When satisfying his physical desires in a manner that is sanctioned by *Halachah,* a Jew must exercise self-control and make moderation the rule. To live a life of self-indulgence and gluttony is, in *Ramban's* words, to be a נָבָל בִּרְשׁוּת הַתּוֹרָה, *a degenerate within the framework of the Torah.*

Man's quest for holiness begins with struggle and striving and ends with reward and gift. The Talmud teaches, "If a man sanctifies himself a bit, they [in Heaven] will sanctify him a great deal. [If he does so] below, they will sanctify him from Above" (*Yoma* 39a).

Thus, *Ramban's* path for life is essentially composed of two ingredients: *emunah* and *kedushah,* faith and sanctity. Pesach, the Festival of spiritual freedom and faith in God, is the ideal time to strengthen oneself in these crucial areas.

The Chametz Prohibitions

Exceptional Stringencies

⇐§ The Torah is more stringent regarding *chametz* than with any other forbidden food. It prohibits not only consumption, but also possession of *chametz* (and even mixtures containing *chametz).* בְּדִיקַת חָמֵץ, *the search for the chametz* on the night before the festival, and בִּיעוּר חָמֵץ, *the disposal of the chametz* the next morning, are predicated on this requirement.

---

1. The Talmud (*Megillah* 6b) states that in a leap year, when the month of Adar is repeated, the holiday of Purim is celebrated in the second Adar, the reason being: מִסְמָךְ גְּאוּלָה לִגְאוּלָה עָדִיף, *it is preferable to juxtapose the redemption [of Purim] to the redemption [of Pesach]. Ramban's* comment lends this explanation added meaning. Purim commemorates the Jews having been saved from the evil designs of Haman who sought their annihilation. Their rescue, as recounted in the Book of *Esther,* was entirely within the order of nature. A seemingly unrelated series of events, which occurred over a period of nine years, brought Esther to the queen's throne, Mordechai to the position of viceroy, Haman and his ten sons to their deaths and the Jews to their salvation. The juxtaposition of Purim to Pesach, which commemorates a redemption marked by miracle upon miracle, underscores the point that "all our happenings and occurrences are miraculous — there is nothing natural in them at all."

Many Scriptural prohibitions against consumption of forbidden foods carry a penalty of *malkos,* lashes. The punishment for willful consumption of *chametz* is *kareis,* spiritual excision. The Sages decreed that the standard laws of nullification do not apply to *chametz;* even the tiniest particle of *chametz* can render an entire mixture forbidden.

The *Arizal* taught that one who is successful in avoiding even inadvertent consumption of the most minute bit of *chametz* during Pesach has earned for himself a special protection against sin for the entire year.

Small wonder that Jews are so meticulous in their pre-Pesach housecleaning and in their zealousness regarding *chametz* during the Festival itself. Through the centuries, many communities have accepted upon themselves added *chumros* (stringencies) which, while not required by *Halachah,* are further safeguards against inadvertent transgression of the *chametz* prohibitions.[1] While customs do vary, all should be respected, for they were originated by the great sages of yesteryear who understood well the deep significance and cosmic nature of every *mitzvah.*

Proof of the Miracle

⋙ The *chametz* prohibitions serve to recall the miraculous nature of the Exodus when. . .

> *Egypt exerted itself upon the people to send them out of the land hurriedly, for they said, "We are all dying!" The people picked up its dough before it became leavened, their leftovers bound up in their garments on their shoulders . . . They baked the dough they took out of Egypt into cakes of matzah, for they could not be leavened, for they were driven from Egypt and could not delay, nor had they made provisions for themselves (Exodus 12:33-34, 39).*

The fact that in the end, the Jews were *driven out* of Egypt and had to leave so hurriedly that they could not even take the time to prepare provisions for the way, made clear for all generations that their deliverance could only have been an act of God. Had they been

---

1. A common example is the custom of many (especially those of Chassidic origin) to refrain from eating *gebrochts* — *matzah* that has come in contact with liquid. This custom is predicated on the possibility that a small bit of flour in the *matzah* was not fully baked and could become *chametz* when coming in contact with liquid.

given the option, the Jews would have chosen to remain just a bit longer, to properly prepare themselves for their journey into the Wilderness. The Egyptians, overcome with dread after the slaying of the firstborn, would not permit them to remain. Thus, the Jews were in the power of their oppressors to the very end and it was God alone Who rescued them (*R' Samson Raphael Hirsch*).

Deeper Meaning

אַךְ בַּיּוֹם הָרִאשׁוֹן תַּשְׁבִּיתוּ שְּׂאֹר מִבָּתֵּיכֶם.

But from the first day shall you eliminate chametz from your premises (*Exodus* 12:15).

שִׁבְעַת יָמִים שְׂאֹר לֹא יִמָּצֵא בְּבָתֵּיכֶם.

Seven days leaven shall not be found in your houses (ibid. 12:19).

וְלֹא יֵרָאֶה לְךָ חָמֵץ.

And chametz shall not be seen with you (ibid. 13:7).

◆§ The medieval commentator *Rabbeinu Bachya* writes:

It is well known that the *chametz* prohibitions allude to the *yetzer hara* (evil inclination), for man is obligated to utilize his *yetzer tov* (good inclination) to subdue his *yetzer hara* . . . The word חָמֵץ, *chametz,* is of the same root as [the word יִתְחַמֵּץ in] כִּי יִתְחַמֵּץ לְבָבִי, *For my heart was in ferment* (*Psalms* 73:21), for when a heart is bent towards wickedness it is referred to by the Sages as *having fermented* [הֶחְמִיץ]. Similarly, fermented wine (vinegar) is called חוֹמֶץ.

Likewise, the Sages state (*Berachos* 17a), "It is obvious and known before You that it is our desire to do Your will — but what prevents us? The 'leaven in the dough.' " The commentators interpret "leaven in the dough" as a reference to the *yetzer hara.*

To the verse, *For He knew our inclination* (*Psalms* 103:14), *Midrash* comments, "Woe to the dough whose Baker bears witness that it is bad" (*Bereishis Rabbah* 34:12).

Therefore, *chametz* was distanced from the Temple Altar, as the Torah prohibited its being used in any offering: *Any meal-offering that you offer to HASHEM may not be made with chametz, for you shall not cause to go up in smoke from any leavening or fruit-honey as a fire-offering to HASHEM* (*Leviticus* 2:11) . . . for the Altar's purpose was to provide atonement and to gain God's favor, but *chametz* does not gain His favor.

Therefore, the Torah required: לֹא יֵרָאֶה, *It [the chametz] shall not be seen (Exodus* 13:7) and לֹא יִמָּצֵא, *It shall not be found* (ibid. 12:19) — [On a homiletical level, this means,] that it [the *yetzer hara*] shall not be seen in your deeds and shall not be found in your thoughts.

. . . All *mitzvos* can be divided into three categories: those verbalized by the mouth; those fulfilled in one's heart; and those performed through deed, as it is written, . . . *it is in* **your mouth** *and in* **your heart** *to do it (Deuteronomy* 30:14). Therefore, the Torah required that *chametz* be nullified in one's heart, [through the formula of *bitul* — see p. 37], corresponding to the *mitzvos* of the heart; that it be removed from one's house or burned,[1] corresponding to the *mitzvos* performed through deed; and that the *"Kol Chamira"* ("Any *Chametz"*) passage be recited,[2] corresponding to the verbal *mitzvos* . . . Thus, the prohibition of *chametz* encompasses all *mitzvos.*

Inasmuch as *chametz* alludes to the *yetzer hara,* we can derive from here that just as the Torah requires that we nullify the *chametz* in our hearts, so, too, are we obligated to nullify the *yetzer hara* in our hearts and not permit it to rule over us . . . and just as we are taught to remove the *chametz* and to search [even] the cracks and crevices for it, so, too, must we search within ourselves for bad thoughts and notions. Just as the search for the *chametz* cannot be done by the light of the sun, the moon, or a torch, but only by the light of a candle,[3] so must the search of the *yetzer hara* be done by the light of the soul, which is called *a candle,* as it is

---

1. While the *Halachah* allows for the *chametz* to be disposed of in any manner, the custom is to burn it (see *Shulchan Aruch* 445:1).

2. Verbal nullification of one's *chametz* is done both following the search for the *chametz* on the night of the fourteenth and following the burning of the *chametz* the next morning. (Note, however, that the texts of these pronouncements are not identical. See p. 37.)

3. *Mishnah Pesachim* 1:1. R' Chaim Vital (disciple of the holy *Arizal*) interpreted this *mishnah* homiletically as an allusion to a Jewish boy's obligations at the time when he becomes a Bar-Mitzvah:

   On the night of the fourteenth — On the eve of the fourteenth year, when a boy enters manhood . . . *we search for the chametz by the light of the candle* — he should utilize the Torah and its commandments to search out and subdue the *yetzer hara* that has been a part of him since birth, as it is written, *since the inclination of man's heart is evil from his youth (Genesis* 8:21).

written, *The soul of man is the candle of* Hashem, *searching all the inward parts*[1] (*Proverbs* 20:27).

(*Kad HaKemach,* Chavel edition, p. 312-313)

Thus, the long and laborious task of making one's home *chametz*-free is far more than mere "spring cleaning." The scrubbing of cabinets and closets helps scrub the chambers of one's heart and purge them of that which distances one from his Creator. The sweep of the broom helps sweep the dust off one's soul so that it can renew itself when the festival of Pesach arrives (R' Shlomo Halberstam of *Bobov*).

A Word to the Weary

⋲§ R' Tzvi Hirsh Feldman (*Tiferes Tzvi*) spoke of the extensive effort that goes into preparing one's home for Pesach:

Each of the Festivals requires extensive preparation, both physical and spiritual. This is especially true of Pesach. Weeks in advance of the Festival, the task of making one's home *chametz*-free has already begun. When the time to sit around the *Seder* table has arrived, virtually everyone is physically drained. If it were up to us, we would recommend that the *Seder* be postponed until we had ample time to rest, so that we could celebrate Pesach amid joy and freedom of both body and spirit.

Yet it was decreed that the *Seder*, with its many requirements, be conducted on *this* night and that we spend much time recounting the details of the Exodus, as we say [in the *Haggadah*], "The more one tells about the Exodus, the more he is praiseworthy."

From this we can derive a fundamental principle, that specifically in a situation where one is tired and drained from his pre-*yom tov* preparations he is to strengthen himself like a lion, to recline in the way of a king and tell about the Exodus at length to his children and to others. It is specifically this sort of situation which is very dear to the Holy One, Blessed is He, for it is through this — when one demonstrates that a myriad of physical factors cannot

---

1. Like a person using a candle to search a dark room, God uses the soul to plumb the inner recesses of man's thoughts (*Metzudos* ad loc.).

prevent him in the least from fulfilling the will of our Father in Heaven — that one can become elevated spiritually in a most profound way.

Avos D'R'Nosson states that "one [deed accomplished] amid pain is greater than two hundred without pain"; the more difficulty one endures in serving his Creator, the greater is his reward. As the Sages state elsewhere (*Avos* 5:22): "In accordance with the effort is the reward."

Chametz and Matzah

❧ The puffed-up *chametz* dough alludes to pride and arrogance, while the flat *matzah* alludes to humility. Arrogance is a most despicable trait, as Scripture states, *Abhorrent to HASHEM are all who are arrogant of heart* (Proverbs 16:5). From another verse, the Sages derive that when God sees an arrogant man, He says, "He and I cannot exist together in the same world" (*Sotah* 5a).

While removal of the *chametz* reminds us to uproot *all* that is negative from within ourselves, it should be cause for reflection regarding this trait in particular.

All the letters in חָמֵץ, *chametz,* and מַצָּה, *matzah,* are identical, except for the ח and the ה. The difference between these two words is dependent on the minute space in the left leg which differentiates a ח from a ה. This tiny difference is symbolic of the difference between *chametz* and *matzah.* Lack of precision in the preparation and baking of *matzah* can quickly turn it into *chametz* (*Alshich*).

Applying this to *chametz*'s symbolism of the *yetzer hara,* we may suggest that the path which one's life takes is often chosen not through major decisions or occurrences, but through subtleties. How often it is that childhood friends of the same background and education drift slowly apart as they mature until they stand worlds apart, one the product of zealousness, the other of complacency.

Erev Pesach

Search and Nullification

◄§ *Bedikas chametz,* the search for *chametz,* should commence at the beginning of the night of 14 Nissan, *Erev Pesach* (the Eve of Pesach). The search is followed by *bitul,* verbal nullification of any *chametz* which one may possess but did not find. The next morning, the *chametz* which has been found during the search and all remaining *chametz* which has not been sold is burned. It is customary to perform *bitul* again after the *chametz* has been destroyed. This second nullification includes any *chametz* that one might still possess, but which he inadvertently did not destroy.[1]

Bitul, by definition, is a declaration of conscious intent by the owner that he considers his *chametz* to be "null," i.e., valueless in his eyes. This declaration frees one from the transgression of owning *chametz* on Pesach, for through *bitul,* any *chametz* that might be present in the individual's domain is now rendered ownerless.[2] A question, therefore, arises: Why is it necessary to search for and dispose of one's *chametz*? Should not nullification alone suffice?

Rashi (Pesachim 2a as elucidated by *Ran)* explains that the need for the search is of Rabbinic origin. The Sages did not rely solely on the device of nullification out of concern that an individual might not utter the *bitul* formula with sincere intent of heart, thus rendering it invalid. *Tosafos* maintains that the obligation to search is based upon an apprehension that the continued presence of *chametz* in one's house may lead to inadvertent consumption.

Why does the search and disposal not suffice without the accompanying nullification? The Talmud (ibid. 6b) explains that the Sages were apprehensive that some *chametz* would be overlooked during the search and subsequently found on Pesach; the owner would then transgress the prohibition against keeping *chametz* unless he destroyed it immediately. Having nullified it, however, no commandment is transgressed if the *chametz* is later found, though, by Rabbinic law, it must be destroyed.

---

1. See Laws section.
2. This is one interpretation of the nature of *bitul* offered by the early commentators.

The Fast of the Firstborn

܀§ *Erev Pesach* is a day of fasting for all firstborn males to commemorate the miracle of the survival of the Jewish firstborn while the Egyptian firstborn were slain by God on the night of the Exodus (*Tur* §470). Common custom is for the firstborn to attend a *seudas mitzvah* (*mitzvah* banquet) such as a *seudas bris, pidyon haben,* or *siyum* celebration upon the completion of a tractate of Talmud or order of Mishnah, and break their fast.

The fast and its accompanying custom is cause for wonder. Miracles are usually cause for celebration, not fasting. Conversely, other fasts in the Jewish calendar cannot be broken by attending a *seudas mitzvah*. What, then, is the nature of this fast?

The purpose of Creation is alluded to in the Torah's opening word, בְּרֵאשִׁית, *In the beginning:*

> בְּרֵאשִׁית — For the sake of the Torah which is called רֵאשִׁית דַּרְכּוֹ, *the beginning of His way* (*Proverbs* 8:22), and for the sake of Israel which is called רֵאשִׁית תְּבוּאָתֹה, *the beginning of His crops* (*Jeremiah* 2:3).   (*Rashi*)

For the sake of the Chosen People who would dedicate their lives on this earth toward the study and fulfillment of God's Torah were heaven and earth created.

As each of the Ten Plagues were brought upon the Egyptians, God's Presence in this world became evermore revealed. The final plague, the slaying of the firstborn, is referred to in the *Haggadah* as גִּלּוּי שְׁכִינָה, *the revelation of God's Presence.* With exacting Providence, at midnight of the fifteenth of Nissan every firstborn Egyptian was slain while every firstborn Jew was spared. It was at that moment that all perceived clearly that it was God and God alone Who created heaven and earth and guides the affairs of this world. And it was at that moment that the Jewish People, the purpose of Creation, became the Chosen Nation (*Nesivos Shalom*).

The Talmud (*Berachos* 35a) states, "Whoever benefits from this world without first reciting a blessing is considered as if [he had transgressed the sin of] benefiting from that which is consecrated to Heaven, as it is written, *The earth is HASHEM's and the fullness thereof*" (*Psalms* 24:1). The purpose of all creation is that it be utilized in the service of God. Therefore, a prerequisite to man's enjoyment of the world's pleasures is that he first declare Who is their Creator and true Owner.

The slaying of the firstborn revealed that *the earth is* HASHEM's *and the fullness thereof.* In commemoration of the firstborn's having been the instrument through which this truth was revealed, all firstborn males are to abstain from the food of this world on *Erev Pesach.* However, this is not the case when they have an opportunity to participate in a *seudas mitzvah.* A *seudas mitzvah,* by definition, is a demonstration that the world is God's and that its pleasures are to be utilized for His service. By breaking their fast at a *seudas mitzvah,* the firstborn bear testimony to God's Presence in this world.[1]

The Afternoon of Erev Pesach

&§ The *Mishnah (Pesachim* 4:1) cites a custom in certain localities during the Temple era of refraining from work on the morning of *Erev Pesach.* After midday, however, labor was forbidden categorically. It was during this afternoon that all Israel offered their Pesach sacrifices in the Temple. As *Talmud Yerushalmi (Pesachim* 4:1) explains, it is not proper that a person go about his work while his Pesach offering is being sacrificed. *Tosafos (Pesachim* 50a) holds that this prohibition is Scriptural, while other authorities *(Meiri, Ritva, Rav)* hold it to be of Rabbinic origin.

P'nei Yehoshua suggests a Scriptural source for this prohibition. In what is known as ''The Chapter of the Festivals,'' the Torah states: *These are the Festivals of* HASHEM, *holy convocations . . . In the first month, on the fourteenth day of the month in the afternoon is the Pesach offering (Leviticus* 23:4-5). The insertion of this verse among the מוֹעֲדִים, *Festivals,* implies that the afternoon of the fourteenth is also a festival when at least some forms of work are prohibited.

It would seem that nowadays, in the absence of the Pesach sacrifice, this prohibition should not apply. However, the *Halachah* states to the contrary *(Shulchan Aruch* 468:1). The commentators explain that it is improper for one to go about his personal business when there is so much to do in the advent of Pesach, more so than for any other festival *(Ravad, Milchamos, Meiri).* As if to anticipate the objection that Succos, too, requires extensive preparation, *Rashi (Pesachim* 50a) adds that Pesach is unique in that the Sages

---

1. For extensive discussion of the nature of this fast and its halachic ramifications, see *Mikra'ei Kodesh* by R' Tzvi Pesach Frank, *Pesach* Vol. II, ch. 22-23.

instructed us to begin the *Seder* as early as possible (after nightfall) so that the children will remain awake (*Pesachim* 106a).

The prohibition against labor during the afternoon of *Erev Pesach* is similar to that of *Chol HaMoed*. [1]

Chametz in the Afternoon

◆§ The Torah prohibits the keeping of *chametz* from midday of *Erev Pesach*. This is derived from the verse, אַךְ בַּיּוֹם הָרִאשׁוֹן תַּשְׁבִּיתוּ שְּׂאֹר מִבָּתֵּיכֶם, *But from the first day shall you eliminate chametz from your premises* (*Exodus* 12:15). The Talmud (*Pesachim* 4b-5b) demonstrates that יוֹם הָרִאשׁוֹן, *the first day,* refers to the day of the Pesach sacrifice, the fourteenth of Nissan. The term אַךְ, *but,* limits this requirement to the second half of the day.

Out of concern that some may not accurately determine the time of midday, the Sages decreed that the prohibition be observed before noon. The *Halachah* follows the opinion of R' Yehudah that the Sages prohibited the consumption of *chametz* two hours before noon, while they prohibited all forms of benefit one hour before noon. Hence, one must sell or give his *chametz* to a gentile, and burn his remaining *chametz* before the final hour before noon.[2]

Another source for the prohibition of *chametz* on this afternoon is the verse, לֹא תִשְׁחַט עַל חָמֵץ דַּם זִבְחִי, *You shall not slaughter the blood of My feast-offering upon leavened food* (*Exodus* 34:25),[3] which prohibits a Pesach sacrifice from being offered until its owners have removed all *chametz* from their possession.

R' Samson Raphael Hirsch sees *matzah* as symbolizing that man's material gains are dependent on God and should be dedicated toward His service. *Chametz* (whose dough rises on its own) symbolizes the opposite: man's tendency to see his worldly acquisitions as the fruits of his own efforts and acumen, and the selfish behavior that such attitudes evoke. The slaughtering of a sacrifice symbolizes the owner's dedicating ("offering") his own self toward service of God. To slaughter the Pesach sacrifice while one still maintains *chametz* in his possession would imply that one can be a spiritual person though he conducts his home and business as if these areas were not in God's domain. To negate such an

---

1. See Laws section.
2. See Laws for the definition of "hour" in halachic terms.
3. An almost identical prohibition is found in *Exodus* 23:18.

implication, the Torah required that all *chametz* be removed before the slaughtering takes place.

קָרְבַּן פֶּסַח /
The Pesach Sacrifice

Symbolisms

◆§ The Pesach sacrifice is unique among Temple offerings in many ways. Four positive commandments and twelve negative commandments were said regarding it.

Sefer HaChinuch (§7) explains that the specific details of the Pesach sacrifice highlight the Jews' freedom and princely status:

> We were specifically commanded to eat it roasted because when served that way it is a dish of kings, fine and delicious. Ordinary people cannot afford such savory meat, and must boil their meat so as to better satiate themselves. Since the Pesach offering is eaten to commemorate our departure from Egypt on our way to becoming a *kingdom of priests and holy nation* (*Exodus* 19:6), we should surely do so in a free and princely fashion.

Moreover, the commandment that prohibits leaving over any part of the Pesach offering until the following morning (*Exodus* 12:10) is a way of accentuating our freedom: "like kings and princes, who never have to save their leftovers from one day to the next" (*Sefer HaChinuch* §8). This idea applies also to the law that forbids anyone outside the predesignated group of a given Pesach offering to eat from it (*Exodus* 12:3-4) — another law unique to this sacrifice. *Sefer HaChinuch* likens this to the practice of kings for whom everything is prepared beforehand in their palace and who dine with a large group of their subjects.

Finally, the Torah prohibits breaking the bones of the Pesach sacrifice (ibid. v. 46), for it is the way of poor people to break the bones of meat to suck the marrow. Such is not the way of kings and princes.

After concluding his explanation of these commandments, *Sefer HaChinuch* sets forth an important principle:

Each year at this time, it is proper for us to perform actions which illustrate the level that we attained [at the time of the Exodus]. By performing these symbolisms, the matter becomes embedded in our souls forever. . .

Know that man is molded by his actions [הָאָדָם נִפְעָל כְּפִי פְּעוּלוֹתָיו]; his heart and thoughts are constantly drawn after the actions which he is involved in, whether for good or for bad. This is true even with regard to a thoroughly wicked person who thinks sinful thoughts all day. If such a person's spirit will be aroused and he will turn his energy and efforts toward the diligent study of Torah and performance of *mitzvos* — even *not* for the sake of Heaven — his heart will quickly become inclined towards good and eventually, he will act for the sake of Heaven [מִתּוֹךְ שֶׁלֹּא לִשְׁמָה בָּא לִשְׁמָה]. Through his deeds, his evil inclination will die, for one's heart is drawn after his actions.

This principle applies as well to a thoroughly righteous person whose heart is upright and perfect and whose desire is Torah and *mitzvos*. If this person will be constantly involved in negative deeds — for example, if the king will force him to undertake a wicked vocation and he will become involved in this vocation all day — then the righteousness of his heart will fade and with time, he will become thoroughly wicked. For it is known and true that הָאָדָם נִפְעָל כְּפִי פְּעוּלוֹתָיו, *man is molded by his actions* (*Sefer HaChinuch* §16).

Two Bloods

"I passed over you and I saw you, behold, the moment was one of love;" (Ezekiel 16:8) — The time had come to [fulfill the] oath that I had sworn to Abraham that I would redeem his children. But they had no mitzvos with which to involve themselves so that [in their merit] they could be redeemed, as it is written, ". . . but you were naked and bare [i.e., devoid of the merit of mitzvos]."

He therefore gave them two mitzvos, the blood of the Pesach offering and the blood of circumcision, for they were circumcised on that night. Thus it is written, "[I passed over you and I saw you] wallowing in your **bloods.**

[בְּדָמַיִךְ]" — in two bloods[1] (*Mechilta* cited by *Rashi* to *Exodus* 12:6).

◆§ *Mechilta* cites the well-known tradition that the Jews in Egypt remained distinct from the Egyptians in their language and names. *Yalkut Shimoni* (§768) adds that they also remained distinct in their manner of dress. Nevertheless, other Midrashic passages make it clear that the Jews, motivated by fear, *did* seek to appear similar to the Egyptians in other ways. After the death of Joseph, the Jews became fearful of losing favor with their hosts. They hoped that by emulating the Egyptians to some degree the status quo would be maintained.

God, however, knew that this course was fraught with spiritual danger, for it could lead to assimilation and the Jews' becoming lost as a people unto themselves. Therefore, *He turned their hearts to hate His people* (*Psalms* 105:25). God, caused the Egyptians to respond with hate to the Jews' overtures. In this way, assimilation was an impossibility and the future of Abraham's progeny was ensured.

At the time of the Exodus, the ministering angel of Egypt declared, "These [the Egyptians] are idol worshipers and those [the Jews] are idol worshipers!" God responded that the Jews who worshiped idols did so only because the intensity of their bondage caused them to become irrational (*Yalkut Shimoni* §234).

In fact, the Jews themselves were at least partially responsible for the degree of persecution they suffered, for, as explained above, their currying favor with the Egyptians brought about the hatred toward them. Therefore, it was necessary for the Jews to rectify this sin by performing two *mitzvos* that would clearly demonstrate their distinctiveness. By openly setting aside and offering a lamb, which the Egyptians worshiped, the Jews demonstrated for all to see that their beliefs were not those of their overlords.[2] And by entering the covenant of Abraham through the performance of *milah*, they

---

1. The verse (*Ezekiel* 16:6) continues: "*And I said to you, 'Through your blood shall you live,' and I said to you, 'Through your blood shall you live.' "*

2. *HaKesav V'HaKaballah* writes:

"The Sages state that the Jews in Egypt had worshiped idols and this prevented their redemption. In His desire to purge them of sin, God commanded that they offer the Pesach sacrifice. By slaughtering the alien gods they had worshiped, they could demonstrate their full repentance.

"Now, when one is to show his unequivocal love for someone, he does not allow fear to prevent him from fulfilling the wishes of that person, even if danger is involved. God therefore commanded that the slaughtering of the idol should include three actions performed in the open streets and markets of Egypt before the eyes of the inhabitants,

demonstrated that physically, as well, they were distinct from the Egyptians.

Once they had made their distinctiveness clear, there was no longer a need for God to arouse the Egyptians toward hatred. Thus, as they prepared to depart Egypt, *the Children of Israel carried out the word of Moses; they borrowed from the Egyptians silver vessels, gold vessels, and garments. HASHEM gave the people favor in the eyes of the Egyptians, and they lent them, so they emptied out Egypt* (*Exodus* 12:35-36) (*Beis HaLevi*).

A Roman's Testimony

◄§ The slaughtering of thousands upon thousands of Pesach sacrifices in the Temple Courtyard on the afternoon of *Erev Pesach* was perhaps the grandest sight witnessed in the Courtyard all year. The service of the Pesach offering is found in *Mishnah Pesachim* (ch. 5) and is recited by many on *Erev Pesach* (see ArtScroll *Pesach Machzor*, p. 46).

Sefer Shevet Yehudah records the testimony of a Roman commissioner (stationed in Jerusalem while the Second Temple stood) regarding the Pesach sacrifice. The testimony was later reprinted in *Siddur Beis Yaakov* by R' Yaakov Emden whose preface to it concludes: "From reading it, we will come to recognize the glory of the House of our God and realize what we have lost due to our sins. Thus, we will pray with a full heart that He return the service of our Holy Temple, speedily and in our time."

Following are excerpts of that testimony:

> When Rosh Chodesh Nissan arrived, emissaries of the king and judges would go throughout Jerusalem's suburbs to announce that whoever owned sheep or goats should bring

---

with no regard for the fact that this would probably enrage the Egyptians. Seeing their gods degraded, the Egyptians were liable to rise up to massacre the Jews, as Moses had told Pharaoh (*Exodus* 8:22): *"If we were to slaughter the deity of Egypt in their sight, would they not stone us?"* Nevertheless, the Jews were to ignore such risks. With open contempt for the Egyptians, they were to bring the lambs to their homes.

"Moreover, the slaughter was to be carried out by large family groups, with great fanfare that would demonstrate fearlessness of the enemy. Along with these two conditions was the requirement that the lamb be consumed with great publicity. Its blood was to be smeared upon the doorposts and lintels of their homes, to the Egyptians' utter despair. In this way, all Egyptian passersby would be able to see that their deity was being consumed. . .

"Despite the risks, God's will was performed without fear. This was a wondrous sign of their full repentance and devotion to God, and their absolute rejection of idolatry."

them to Jerusalem so that there would be enough for the throngs of Festival pilgrims to sacrifice and eat . . .

The people would quickly comply. The animals were forded across a stream near Jerusalem to cleanse them. The fleecy sheep and clean goats that came up from the stream were a marvelous sight to behold . . . The flocks making their way to the city were so numerous that they covered the mountainside, hiding the grasses. The slopes appeared white like snow.

On the tenth of Nissan everyone went to purchase their Pesach offerings.[1] The Jews enacted an ordinance forbidding anyone from asking his neighbor to step aside and allow him to precede him on line to purchase his animal — even if the last person on line was King David or Solomon! I asked the *Kohanim* (Priests) about this and they explained to me that this law was to demonstrate that the moments when one is serving God or preparing to serve Him are not times for personal pride; all Jews are beloved in the eyes of their Master.

On the fourteenth of the month, *Kohanim* would ascend to a high tower in the Temple and sound three silver trumpets. Then they would announce: "Nation of God, hearken! The time has come to slaughter the Pesach sacrifice for the sake of the One Who domiciled His Name in this great and holy House." When the people would hear this announcement, they would don their Festival garments. From midday and on, when the sacrifice could be offered, was a festival for the Jews.

Twelve *Leviim* (Levites) stood outside the gates of the Courtyard holding silver wands in their hands, while twelve other *Leviim* with golden wands stood within the gates. Those outside were responsible for order; they had to ensure that the people did not push one another or enter in unruly crowds, which could lead to strife. The *Leviim* who were inside had to ensure that those who had already sacrificed their offerings would leave in an orderly fashion. When the Courtyard was filled, the gates of the Courtyard were locked. [The Pesach sacrifice was slaughtered in three shifts.][2]

---

1. The Torah requires that the Pesach sacrifice be inspected for blemishes for four days prior to its being offered on the fourteenth of Nissan. See *Pesachim* 96a.
2. Much of what follows appears in the fifth chapter of *Mishnah Pesachim*.

At the site of the slaughtering, one would come upon rows and rows of *Kohanim*,[1] and in their hands were silver bowls and golden bowls. One row was altogether of silver, the next row was altogether of gold. [This was done to enhance the beauty of the *mitzvah*.] The *Kohen* at the head of each line would receive a bowl with the blood of the sacrifice and would pass it on to the next in line, and so on, until it reached the Altar. The blood would then be thrown upon the Altar, after which the *Kohen* would return the empty bowl to the one next in line, and so on, until it reached the head of the line. Thus, each *Kohen* was receiving a full bowl and returning an empty bowl [at the very same moment that his fellow *Kohanim* were doing the same]. This back-and-forth procedure never became confused; the *Kohanim* were so adept at their work that the bowls moved back and forth as swiftly as an arrow shot from an archer's bow.

. . . Two *Kohanim* stood on high pedestals. At the commencement of each shift, they would sound a blast on their silver trumpets as a signal to the *Leviim* on the platform to begin the *Hallel* with singing and music. During the service, the owners of the sacrifices would also recite *Hallel*.

. . . When the service had ended, they would leave joyously with a happy heart, like one who went to battle and emerged victorious . . . The ovens in which they roasted the offering's meat was set outside their doorways. I have been told that this was done to publicize their beliefs [לְפַרְסֵם הָאֱמוּנָה] and due to the joy of the Festival. [At night,] they would eat the roasted meat amid *Hallel* and song and their voices could be heard in the distance. . .

The Seder Night

Of Another World

⊷§ The Chassidic master, R' Mordechai of Lechovitch, would say that a Jew must have faith that, indeed, he has faith. Even if a Jew experiences times when his *emunah* (faith) seems clouded with

---

1. The involvement of so many *Kohanim* in this service was in fulfillment of the verse, *The king's glory is in the multitudes of people* (Proverbs 14:28).

doubt, he should realize that in the depths of his soul his faith remains intact — only its radiance has become obscured.

This truth is most evident on the night of the *Seder*, which is conducted not only by observant Jews, but also by scores who otherwise demonstrate little connection to Jewish tradition.

In the words of R' Zalman Sorotzkin:

Each one of us knows how uplifted he feels on this night, when he sits at the *Seder* table and relates to his children and all assembled of God's awesome might and of the wonders He performed when He took our forefathers out of Egypt.

It is common to see even non-observant people suddenly become transformed on the *Seder* night; they arrange a *Seder*, recount the details of the Exodus, and eat *matzah* and *maror*. One is moved to ask: *Why is this night different from all other nights?*

When I was in Russia, I once found myself in an area that was inhabited by non-observant Jews. I was told of a family living there that ate *treife* (non-kosher food) all year long, but when Pesach arrived, they would buy new pots and pans so that they could eat not only *matzah* and *maror*, but kosher meat as well! When Pesach ended, the kitchen returned to its usual, unkosher status.

I myself knew a man who ate *treife* all year long, but on Pesach was exacting in his concern over the most minute crumb of *chametz!* This man would frequently approach the rabbi of his city with Festival-related halachic questions.

In the annals of our history, we find that Jews in Spain, who out of fear abandoned the ways of their forefathers, hid in forests and caves in order to conduct a *Seder* out of sight of the wicked Inquisitors (may their names be blotted out).

We have heard that in the days when the *Yevsektzia* (Jewish Communists) held real power in Russia and would persecute any party member who displayed the slightest trace of Jewish faith or observance, many members (and even some *Yevsektzia* leaders themselves) would conduct the *Seder* in secret, at the risk of their lives. And so we ask again: *Why is this night different from all other nights?*

The answer must be אִם אֵינְהוּ חָזוּ לֹא חָזוּ, מַזְלַיְיהוּ חָזוּ, *If they did not perceive it, their essential nature perceived it*[1] (*Megillah* 3a). On this night, the miracles and wonders of the Exodus filter through the subconscious of every Jew and create a turmoil within his soul. Each Jew, whether he realizes it or not, sees *himself* as having actually been redeemed from Egypt.[2] Each Jew's soul is illuminated with a Heavenly light and bursts with the yearnings of David, who said, *My soul yearns, indeed it pines, for the courtyards of* HASHEM, *my heart and my flesh will sing joyously to the living God* (*Psalms* 84:3).

In *Bircas HaMazon* on the *Seder* night, we say, *The Compassionate One! May He cause us to inherit the day which is completely good, that everlasting day, the day when the righteous will sit with crowns on their heads, enjoying the reflection of God's majesty — and may our portion be with them!* On no other occasion but the *Seder* do we recite this prayer. On this night, we experience a semblance of the World to Come. Thus are we inspired to pray that we "inherit that day" — and we add a prayer that "our portion be with them," for on this night our souls truly yearn for a life that is spiritual and pure (*HaDei'ah V'Hadibur*).

"Leil Shimurim"

◌§ The *Seder* night is known as לֵיל שִׁמֻּרִים, *Leil Shimurim*. The term שִׁמֻּרִים appears twice in a single verse in *Exodus* where *Rashi* offers respective interpretations:

לֵיל שִׁמֻּרִים הוּא לַה׳ לְהוֹצִיאָם מֵאֶרֶץ מִצְרַיִם, הוּא הַלַּיְלָה הַזֶּה לַה׳ שִׁמֻּרִים לְכָל בְּנֵי יִשְׂרָאֵל לְדֹרֹתָם.

*It is a night of anticipation [*שִׁמֻּרִים*] for* HASHEM *to take them out of the land of Egypt; it was this night for* HASHEM *a protection [*שִׁמֻּרִים*] for all the Children of Israel for their generations* (*Exodus* 12:42).

---

1. *Rashi* to *Megillah* 3a explains that every person is designated an angel that represents him in Heaven. This is the real meaning of a person's מַזָּל, *mazal*. However, the term is sometimes used to refer to a person's essential nature or subconscious, as is the case here.
2. In *Mishnah Pesachim* (10:5 and quoted in the *Haggadah*) we read: "In every generation, it is one's duty to regard himself as if he personally had gone out of Egypt."

To the first שִׁמֻּרִים in the verse, *Rashi* comments:

"A night of anticipation — For the Holy One, Blessed is He, was waiting for and anticipating this night when He could fulfill His promise to take them out of the land of Egypt."

R' David Feinstein (*Kol Dodi al HaTorah*) writes that the term *anticipation* suggests that God was watching and waiting anxiously, as it were, for the most appropriate time to take the Jews out of Egypt. This implies that there had been no fixed time for the redemption; had there been, God would have waited patiently until it came, instead of watching anxiously to see whether or not *now* would be the time.

Thus, the four hundred years of exile and servitude that God had foretold to Abraham was not inflexible. Under certain conditions, the time could be shortened. This is why God "watched" for the most propitious time.[1]

Just as the Egyptian exile was flexible, the duration of the current exile is also not fixed. This explains why there have been so many unfulfilled predictions by the Torah giants throughout the centuries that the redemption would come at one time or another. The times they predicted were indeed suitable for redemption, but the people were not worthy of it.

The Talmud (*Sanhedrin* 98a) relates that someone once asked the Messiah when he would come. "Today," was the answer, but the Messiah did not come that day.

The next day, the questioner asked the prophet Elijah, harbinger of redemption, "Why did he lie to me yesterday? He said that he would come 'today' but he didn't come!"

Elijah answered, "He didn't lie. He said 'today,' in the sense of the Psalmist: *Even today, if we but heed his call"* (*Psalms* 95:7). The time was right but the people were not worthy.

It is in our power, and is therefore our obligation both as a people and as individuals, to make ourselves worthy of redemption at the earliest possible time.

---

1. Indeed, the Egyptian exile lasted two hundred and ten years, for God, in His compassion, calculated the four hundred years from the birth of Isaac.

Night of Protection

◆§ To the second use of שִׁמֻּרִים in the above-cited verse, *Rashi* comments: *"A protection* — [A night which] is protected against destructive spiritual forces, as is written [with regard to this night]: *'And He will not permit the destroyer to enter your homes to smite' "* (*Exodus* 12:23).

Rashi (12:22) identifies the *mashchis*, destroyer, as destructive spiritual forces that are prevalent during the hours of night. *Rashi* interprets *mashchis* this way because God Himself smote the Egyptian firstborn, without the involvement of any emissary. Therefore, *mashchis* could only refer to those forces that are prevalent on every night, rather than on this night alone.[1]

The recital of *Shema* immediately before retiring [קְרִיאַת שְׁמַע עַל הַמִּטָּה][2] serves as a שְׁמִירָה, *protection*, against the dangers of the night (*Zohar; Shulchan Aruch; Shelah*). In concluding the laws of the *Seder*, *Rama* (481:2) states: "It is customary to recite only the first chapter of *Shema* and omit the additional supplications which are usually recited as an [added] shield, for it is לֵיל שִׁמֻּרִים, *a night of protection* from harmful forces." *Mishnah Berurah* (§4) adds that one should recite the *HaMapil* benediction. If one recited *Ma'ariv* before dark, he should say all three chapters of *Shema* before midnight to fulfill the requirement of reciting *Shema* at night.

For All Generations

◆§ R' Zalman Sorotzkin (*HaDei'ah V'HaDibur*) expounds upon the above verse homiletically:

It is a night that was safeguarded [שִׁמֻּרִים] *unto* HASHEM — this night was safeguarded [i.e. set aside[3]] for the spiritual, for the revelation of the Divine Presence and for prophecy. *To take them out of the land of Egypt* — with signs and

---

1. See *Ramban*'s explanation of *Rashi*.

2. Not to be confused with the *Shema* recited as part of *Ma'ariv* to fulfill the Scriptural requirement of reciting *Shema* each day and each night. (See further in text.)

3. The *Midrash* (*Shemos Rabbah* 18:12) explains *Leil Shimurim* as a *night set aside* for miraculous salvation of the righteous throughout the generations. The poem וּבְכֵן וַיְהִי בַּחֲצִי הַלַּיְלָה (*It Came to Pass at Midnight*) found in the *Haggadah* enumerates thirteen events that occurred on this night. See also the לֵיל שִׁמֻּרִים *piyut* recited by some on the first night of Pesach (ArtScroll *Machzor* p. 68).

wonders. *This night is for HASHEM* — to acquire faith in God and bask in the splendor of His Presence. And this is not only for those of lofty spiritual stature; rather, it is *for all the Children of Israel.* Anyone in whom even a tiny spark of spirituality still exists can become uplifted on this night and strengthen himself with faith in God. This is said not only for the generation that departed Egypt. Rather, it is *for their generations.* The spiritual aura of the Exodus returns each year. On this night, every Jew who has not totally severed his connection with his people and with his Father in Heaven yearns to cling to the One Above and to emulate His ways.

Like Yom Kippur

⋖§ The Chassidic masters would say: לֵיל שְׁמֻרִים הוּא כְּיוֹם הַכִּפּוּרִים, *"Leil Shimurim is like the day of Yom Kippur."* Both Yom Kippur and the *Seder* night are times of intense spirituality. It is noteworthy that on both these occasions there is a custom for married men to don a tunic-like garment called a *kittel,* whose white color is reminiscent of angels.[1]

On Yom Kippur, we attain *dveikus,* attachment to God, through יִרְאָה, awe. On the *Seder* night, we attain *dveikus* through אַהֲבָה, *love,* a higher level of service.

As mentioned above,[2] *Sefer HaChinuch,* in discussing the Pesach sacrifice, sets forth the principle הָאָדָם נִפְעָל כְּפִי פְּעוּלוֹתָיו, *man is molded by his actions.* Physical performance of a *mitzvah* binds one's soul with the *mitzvah's* essence.

On Yom Kippur, we abstain from eating, drinking, and other forms of physical enjoyment. Aside from being a source of atonement, such abstention raises one to the level of angels who do not engage in, nor have any need for, such pleasures. On the *Seder* night, by conducting ourselves in a manner of חֵרוּת, *freedom,*[3] and executing various

---

1. The custom of wearing a *kittel* on the *Seder* night is mentioned in *Mishnah Berurah* 472:13. An additional reason for wearing the *kittel* on Yom Kippur and on the *Seder* night is that burial shrouds are white. Thus, the *kittel* reminds us of the vulnerability of human life. On Yom Kippur, this inspires repentance, while on the *Seder* night, it serves as a reminder that the royal nature of the evening should not bring one to haughtiness.

2. P 42.

3. Though all year long one should minimize displaying beautiful vessels, as a remembrance of the Temple's destruction [זֵכֶר לְחוּרְבָּן], such is not the case with the *Seder* night when this serves to enhance the aura of חֵרוּת, *freedom (Mishnah Berurah* 472:6).

mitzvos which symbolize this theme, we reveal within ourselves our true status as בְּנֵי מְלָכִים, *princes* (*Shabbos* 67a). It is on this night that we have the ability to rise above the level of angels as a *kingdom of priests and a holy nation* (*Exodus* 19:6).

The Term "Seder"

◆§ The word *Seder* means *order*. As applied to the first night of Pesach,[1] the term indicates that the rituals and texts of this night were arranged by the Sages in a definitive *order* to which one must adhere. Moreover, every detail in this *order* is significant; each custom and ritual is laden with deep and esoteric meaning. Though we have no understanding of their deep intent, we can rest assured that by adhering to the Sages' instructions and experiencing the *Seder* according to the procedure which they formulated, we merit to become exalted and sanctified with an awesome spiritual light[2] (*Sefer HaToda'ah*).

Maharal writes that the *order* of this night alludes to the fact that all the happenings of Jewish history, from the Exodus until today, are a part of the *order* of Israel's destiny, brought about by God through *hashgachah pratis*, Divine Providence. Nothing occurs haphazardly and nothing is left to chance.

Order for the Year

◆§ Alluded to in the term *Seder* is the fact that the day of the week on which Pesach begins provides an *order* for all the holidays of the Jewish calendar.

There is a system of arrangement of the letters of the *Aleph-Beis* (Hebrew alphabet) in which letters from opposite ends of the *Aleph-Beis* are paired and exchanged. The first letter, א, is paired with the last letter, ת, forming the couplet א״ת; the second letter, ב, is paired with the ש, forming ב״ש; and so on. This arrangement of letters is called א״ת בַּ״שׁ, *At-Bash*.[3]

If one knows the day of the week on which the first day of Pesach falls, he can determine on what days the other holidays fall by means

---

1. In the Diaspora, the first two nights.

2. The laws of the *Seder* are detailed in *Shulchan Aruch* Ch. 472-484 and are discussed extensively in *The Kol Dodi Haggadah* by Rabbi David Feinstein.

3. This system is used extensively in kabbalistic literature.

of the first six couplets of *At-Bash*. The first letter of each couplet stands for the number of the day of Pesach, while the second letter of the couplet stands for the initial of the holiday that falls on that day of the week:

א״ת — The first day of Pesach (א) falls on the same day of the week as תִּשְׁעָה בְּאָב, *the Ninth of Av*.[1]

ב״ש — The second day of Pesach (ב) falls on the same day of the week as שָׁבוּעוֹת, *Shavuos*.

ג״ר — The third day of Pesach (ג) falls on the same day of the week as ראֹשׁ הַשָּׁנָה, *Rosh Hashanah*.

ד״ק — The fourth day of Pesach (ד) falls on the same day of the week as קְרִיאַת הַתּוֹרָה, lit., *Reading of the Torah*, an allusion to *Simchas Torah*, when the year's Torah reading is completed.

ה״צ — The fifth day of Pesach (ה) falls on the same day of the week as צוֹם כִּפּוּר, *Fast of Yom Kippur*.

ו״פ — The sixth day of Pesach (ו) falls on the same day of the week as the previous פּוּרִים, *Purim*.　　　　(*Shulchan Aruch* 428:3)

Keywords

⊱ A series of סִמָּנִים , *keywords*, in rhyme leads us from one stage of the Seder to the next. Its authorship is ascribed to either *Rashi* or *R' Shmuel of Falaise*, one of the authors of *Tosafos*. Aside from its convenience as a memory device, this formula has been given various deep interpretations. *Yesod V'Shoresh HaAvodah* writes: "Great and awesome fundaments are alluded to in these words." Accordingly, many people recite the appropriate keyword before performing the ritual to which it applies.

The sixteenth-century commentator R' Moshe Alshiech (*Alshich*) offered the following interpretation of the סִמָּנִים (the plain meaning of each keyword appears in parentheses):

קַדֵּשׁ, Kaddeish (*Sanctify* the day with the recitation of *Kiddush.*)

וּרְחַץ, Urechatz (*Wash* the hands before eating *Karpas*.)

Sanctify yourself in that which is permissible to you,[2] and *cleanse* (*wash*) your soul of imperfection.

כַּרְפַּס, Karpas (Eat a *vegetable* dipped in salt water.)

The letters of כַּרְפַּס can be rearranged in the following way: כ פ רס. In the Hebrew language, the letters ס and שׂ are sometimes

---

1. This is one source for the custom to eat an egg, traditionally eaten by mourners, at the Seder as a commemoration of the Temple's destruction (*Rama* 476:2).

2. See p. 31.

interchanged. Thus, one should serve one's own needs with a כַּף, spoon; i.e., with the minimum. However, one should serve the רָשׁ, poor man, generously.

יַחַץ, Yachatz (Break the middle matzah. Put away the larger half for afikoman.)

Break your food in half. Keep one half for yourself and give the other half to the poor.

מַגִּיד, Maggid (Tell the details of the Exodus.)

רָחְצָה, Rachtzah (Wash the hands prior to the meal.)

Tell others (i.e. influence them) of the importance of cleansing their souls.

מוֹצִיא, Motzi (Recite the blessing of HaMotzi [Who brings forth. . .] over the matzah as a food.)

מַצָּה, Matzah (Recite the blessing for the mitzvah of eating matzah on this night.)

Bring forth (motzi) and reveal your yetzer tov (good inclination) which is likened to matzah.[1]

מָרוֹר, Maror (Recite the blessing for the eating of the bitter herbs.)

כּוֹרֵךְ, Koreich (Eat the sandwich [wrapping] of matzah with maror.)

Wrap your yetzer tov (good inclination, represented by the matzah) together with your yetzer hara (evil inclination, represented by the bitter herbs), for the Sages (Mishnah Berachos 9:5) teach that one should serve God with both his good and evil inclinations.[2]

שֻׁלְחָן עוֹרֵךְ, Shulchan Oreich (The table is prepared with the festive meal.)

צָפוּן, Tzafun (Eat the Afikoman which has been hidden throughout the Seder.)

One who follows the path outlined above will have a table [of reward] prepared and hidden away for him in the World to Come, as it is written: How abundant is Your goodness which You have hidden away for those who fear You . . . (Psalms 31:20).

בָּרֵךְ, Bareich (Recite Bircas HaMazon, Grace after Meals.)

הַלֵּל, Hallel (Recite the Hallel Psalms of praise.)

נִרְצָה, Nirtzah (Pray that God accept our observance and speedily send the Messiah.)

. . . and his blessings and praises of God in the World to Come will find favor (i.e. be accepted) before Him.

---

1. See p. 36.

2. The true function of the yetzer hara is to elevate man by providing him with a challenge to overcome. Furthermore, even man's baser instincts must be harnessed to serve God (see Rabbeinu Yonah's commentary to Berachos 54a).

Don't Despair

☙ As mentioned above, the Jewish people underwent an incredible spiritual transformation at the time of the Exodus. From the forty-ninth level of spirtual impurity, they rose to the level of prophets at the Splitting of the Sea.

Spiritual refinement is, generally speaking, initiated by man. God, as it were, beckons us, "Open for Me an opening like the eye of a needle and I will open for you an opening like that of a huge hallway." Man is to take the initial step toward God; having done so, he is assured of the Heavenly assistance needed for a complete return to the proper path. This sort of process is referred to in Kabbalistic literature as אִתְעֲרוּתָא דִלְתַתָּא, an awakening initiated from below [i.e. by man].

However, such was not the process at the time of the Exodus. Only an אִתְעֲרוּתָא דִלְעֵילָא, an awakening initiated from Above, could have rescued the Jews from the morass into which they had fallen. Having been granted this gift, the Jews were then able to engage in their own spiritual striving, so that they could maintain the awesome level to which they had been raised.

This process is alluded to in the first two of the סִמָּנִים, keywords: קַדֵּשׁ, Kaddeish — Initially, God sanctified us from above. וּרְחַץ, U'Rechatz — only then were we able to cleanse ourselves.

These two opening keywords provide not only a seder, order, for this night but for one's lifetime as well. No Jew should ever consider himself beyond hope, beyond the point of return to his spiritual roots and the ways of his forefathers. Just as God provided the Jews in Egypt with an awakening which He initiated, so, too, does He present every one of us with situations and circumstances that can provide the impetus toward real spiritual change. It is for us to recognize such opportunities and not allow them to slip by (R' Yitzchok Kirzner). [1]

The pages that follow focus on the Seder's primary components.

---

1. As mentioned above, many of the Torah's commandments are intended as a זֵכֶר לִיצִיאַת מִצְרַיִם, remembrance of the Exodus from Egypt. In recalling the Exodus, a Jew should remind himself never to despair from spiritual striving, no matter how dismal his present situation (Pri Tzaddik, Pesach §24).

"One aspect of pure Jewish faith is that God, the Master of Compassion, has compassion for all Jewish souls and seeks their perfection, so that they can attain their

סִפּוּר יְצִיאַת מִצְרַיִם /
Recounting the Details of the Exodus

At the time [when the details of the Exodus are being recounted], the Holy One, Blessed is He, assembles His Heavenly retinue and says to them, "Come and hear how My children recount My praise and rejoice in My having redeemed them."

(Zohar, Parashas Bo)

"And You Shall Tell Your Son. . ."

◈§ Rambam (Hilchos Chametz U'Matzah 7:1) writes:

It is a positive Scriptural commandment to recount on the night of the fifteenth of Nissan the miracles and wonders that were done for our ancestors in Egypt, as it is written, Remember this day on which you departed from Egypt (Exodus 13:3), [implying verbal remembrance] just as is stated [regarding the Sabbath], Remember the Sabbath day (ibid. 20:8). And from where do we derive that this is to be done on the night of the fifteenth?[1] The Torah states (ibid. 13:8): And you shall tell [וְהִגַּדְתָּ] your son on that day, saying: 'It is because of **this** [that HASHEM acted on my behalf when I left Egypt.' The pronoun זֶה, this, implies something tangible, that this be done] — at a time when matzah and maror lie before you. Even for one who has no son, and even if all those assembled are great of wisdom, there is an obligation to recount the details of the Exodus. The more one

---

true purpose. History has shown how God brings about a myriad of happenings so that great things can come about specifically through people who find themselves in difficult straits. . . . Even if someone has sinned greatly, Heaven forfend, God has ways through which to purify him" (Sefer Eitzos V'Hadrachos by R' Yaakov Greenwald).

1. In the Diaspora, all mitzvos which apply on the night of the fifteenth apply (by Rabbinic decree) on the night of the sixteenth as well (Rama 481:2).

2. The term הַגָּדָה, Haggadah, is derived from וְהִגַּדְתָּ, And you shall tell.

elaborates on that which transpired, the more he is praise-worthy.

It is important to note that men and women are equally obligated in all the *mitzvos* of the *Seder* (*Shulchan Aruch* 472:14).[1] A woman who is preoccupied with tending to her children or preparing the meal is, nevertheless, not exempt from these require-ments.

What is the minimum that one must recite to have discharged his or her obligation of סִפּוּר יְצִיאַת מִצְרַיִם?

In the Mishnah, we read: "Rabban Gamliel used to say: 'Whoever has not explained the following three things on Pesach has not fulfilled his obligation, namely: [the] *Pesach* [offering], *matzah*, and *maror*' " (*Mishnah Pesachim* 10:5). *Rambam* (*Hilchos Chametz U'Matzah* 7:5) understands the "obligation" to which Rabban Gamliel refers as that of recounting the details of the Exodus. The Chofetz Chaim (*Mishnah Berurah* 473:64), therefore, rules that women must, at the very minimum, be present from the reading of Rabban Gamliel's statement until the blessing which precedes the second cup.[2] He adds that it is customary for women to also be present for the recounting of the Ten Plagues, when the miracles of the Exodus are enumerated.

Rama (473:6 citing *Kolbo* and *Maharil*) writes that the *Haggadah* should be read or explained in a language which all present will understand. *Rama* (who lived in the sixteenth century) adds that a sage of an earlier generation, *R' Y. of Lundrei* (London), had translated the *Haggadah* into his native tongue!

As with all *mitzvos*, a child who is old enough to understand the significance of the *Seder* rituals should perform them (*Shulchan Aruch* 472:15). With regard to the *Seder*, we find the unusual statement that candies should be distributed to the young children

---

1. Women are generally exempt from מִצְוַת עֲשֵׂה שֶׁהַזְּמַן גְּרָמָה, *positive commandments which are time related*. The Talmud (*Pesachim* 43b), through Scriptural exegesis, derives that eating *matzah* on the *Seder* night is an exception to this rule. With regard to the Rabbinic *mitzvah* of *arba kosos* (the Four Cups), the Talmud (ibid. 108a) states that women are obligated "for they too were included in the miracle." The commentators cite the Aggadic teaching that "in the merit of righteous women were our ancestors redeemed from Egypt" (*Sotah* 11b). Women are likewise obligated in all other *mitzvos* of this night, though they are not required to recline, for such was never their custom (*Shulchan Aruch* 472:4).

2. They must also recite the *Hallel* which follows the drinking of the third cup (*Tosafos*, *Succah* 38a ד"ה מי).

so that they should not fall asleep (*Pesachim* 109a cited by *Shulchan Aruch* 472:16).[1]

The Torah expresses the obligation of סִפּוּר יְצִיאַת מִצְרַיִם with the command, *And you shall tell your son . . .* As explained above, the *Seder* night is one of *emunah*, faith, a time most opportune for absorbing the basic principles of our faith and instilling them into others. The parent-child relationship is the primary means through which faith is implanted in the next generation. When a father relates to his son the miracles of the Exodus as taught to him by *his* father and his Torah teachers as part of an unbroken chain that reaches until the generation of the Exodus who witnessed these wonders, the child's soul becomes united with the faithful of every generation.[2] This is the primary *means* of instilling faith. The primary *time* is the *Seder* night "when the *matzah* and *maror* lie before you" (*Nesivos Shalom*).

The Four Questions

◆§ The asking of the Four Questions is a necessary prelude to the reciting of the *Haggadah*. Scripture's first mention of the recounting of the Exodus narrative is in response to a son's question (*Exodus* 12:26). The point at which the second cup has been poured is most appropriate for the questions, for this second cup (as opposed to the cup of *Kiddush*) serves to arouse the child's[3] curiosity (*Rashi, Rashbam*).

An oft-quoted comment regarding the Four Questions is that of *Abarbanel*, who points out that the first two questions refer to *Seder* features which relate to bondage (*matzah and maror*), while the last two refer to symbolisms of freedom (dipping foods and reclining). The questions highlight the seeming contradiction of alluding to both bondage and freedom at the same time.

The basic structure of the Four Questions is found in *Mishnah Pesachim* (10:4). Three of the four questions found there are recited to this day. The fourth is not because it was applicable only during the Temple era when the Pesach sacrifice was offered: "Why is this

---

1. The Chofetz Chaim is critical of those who send their children to sleep immediately after they recite the *Mah Nishtanah* (Four Questions). The point of having the children ask these questions is so that they can be given a response. At the very least, they should remain at the table until after the next passage [. . .עֲבָדִים הָיִינוּ לְפַרְעֹה בְּמִצְרָיִם] is read and explained (*Mishnah Berurah* 472:15).

2. See *Ramban* to *Deuteronomy* 4:9.

3. If no children are present, an adult recites the Four Questions. This includes situations where all present are Torah scholars or where one is conducting the *Seder* alone (*Shulchan Aruch* 473:7).

night different. . . On all nights we eat meat roasted, stewed, or cooked, but on this night only roasted." In place of this question, we ask, ". . . On all other nights we eat either sitting or reclining, but on this night — we all recline."

When putting forth a series of questions it is logical to express them in ascending order of difficulty. Thus, it would seem that the question of why "we all recline" is the most perplexing of all.

In ancient times, it was customary for the upper class to recline on couches while eating. During the celebration of our freedom, it is appropriate for us to conduct ourselves in this way. This, however, is most perplexing to the child. How can we, who are mired in this deep and bitter *galus* (exile), act as if we had been redeemed? Are we not *required* to always be mindful of the fact that, indeed, we are in exile?

Our answer to the child is that, as mentioned above, when God redeemed us from Egypt, He took us out לְחֵרוּת עוֹלָם, *to eternal freedom*. We had been mired in the depths of impurity, to the point that *had not the Holy One, Blessed is He, taken our fathers out of Egypt, then we, our children, and our children's children would have remained enslaved to Pharaoh in Egypt* (from the *Haggadah's* response to the Four Questions). We would have remained enslaved in a spiritual sense, for had we remained in Egypt any longer our souls would have sunk to the point of no return.

Never again would we face this danger, for upon redemption, we became a nation of Torah. Adherence to Torah ensures our *eternal freedom* in a spiritual sense and this freedom is cause for real celebration.

The Talmud (*Nedarim* 81a) states that the generation at the time of the Destruction of the First Temple was guilty of "not reciting the [required] blessing on the Torah prior to learning." R' Aharon Kotler (*Mishnas R' Aharon* I, p. 26) explains: "They believed in Torah and *mitzvos* and fulfilled their religious obligations, including involvement and toil in Torah study, but they failed to appreciate the inestimable value of Torah, that without it there is no purpose whatsoever to creation and that the whole eternal purpose of life can be fulfilled only through Torah. Therefore, they failed to recognize the magnitude of the obligation to offer praise [to God] for the Torah [by reciting the blessing on the Torah]. Because of this, they lacked the benefit of the full spiritual light that radiates from Torah."[1]

---

1. See Overview to ArtScroll *Tishah B'Av* book.

The more one appreciates the gift of Torah, the more he perceives the significance of the redemption that brought our people to the foot of Mount Sinai to receive the Torah. Therefore, attainment of wisdom is *not* a reason to refrain from recounting the wonders of the Exodus. To the contrary, *even if we were all men of wisdom, understanding, experience, and knowledge of the Torah, it would still be an obligation upon us to tell about the Exodus from Egypt. The more one tells about the Exodus, the more he is praiseworthy (Haggadah)*.

The Response to the Wicked Son

◆§ The second half of the verse from which the commandment to recount the details of the Exodus is derived serves as the response to the wicked son mentioned in the *Haggadah*.

> The wicked one — what does he say? "Of what purpose is this work to you?" He says, "to you," thereby excluding himself. By excluding himself from the community of believers, he denies the basic principle of Judaism. Therefore, blunt his teeth and tell him: בַּעֲבוּר זֶה עָשָׂה ה' לִי בְּצֵאתִי מִמִּצְרָיִם, *[And you shall tell your son on that day, saying:] 'It is because of this that HASHEM acted on my behalf when I left Egypt.' 'On my behalf,'* but not on his behalf — had he been there, he would not have been redeemed.

The basic difference between the wise son and the wicked son is that the wise son is willing to perform the *mitzvos* though he does not yet understand them. Of course, he seeks to know the reasons behind their performance. For the moment, however, the fact that his father has taught him that such is Jewish tradition is sufficient. Not so the wicked son, who declares, *"to you,"* but not *"to me,"* meaning, "I will not do what I cannot comprehend."

In all probability, the wicked son is well acquainted with the story of the Exodus and all its wonders. However, his heart is drawn after those who propound their own reasons for a given *mitzvah* and then declare the reason — and hence, the *mitzvah* — irrelevant to modern times.

The Pesach sacrifice is not in the category of a *chok*, a *mitzvah* whose reason is hidden from us. Its purpose was to publicly renounce the Egyptians and their faith by slaughtering the lamb which they worshiped.[1] The wicked son contends that in the modern world,

---

1. See p. 43.

where civilization is monotheistic, this *mitzvah* is outdated. He clothes himself in self-righteousness, insisting that, of course, he wishes to serve God — but not according to the way of his fathers! *"To you,"* but not *"to me."*

What is our response? We "blunt his teeth" by explaining the wicked son's basic error in his understanding of *mitzvos*. True, there is a known reason for almost all of the 613 commandments, but the true depth of God's intent in any given *mitzvah* is beyond our comprehension.

As an example, let us take the *mitzvah* of *matzah*. In the *Haggadah* we say, "*Matzah* — Why do we eat this unleavened bread? Because the dough of our fathers did not have time to become leavened before the King of kings, the Holy One, Blessed is He, revealed Himself to them and redeemed them." This only serves to explain why *we* merited this *mitzvah* (as the text indicates: *Matzah* — Why do *we* eat . . .). It cannot possibly be the primary reason for the *mitzvah* itself, for the Torah preceded Creation, and the Patriarchs fulfilled the entire Torah, including the eating of *matzah* on Pesach.[1] In fact, the Jews themselves ate *matzah* on the night of the Exodus *before* they departed the land with their unleavened dough on their shoulders!

It was not the redemption that brought about the *mitzvos* of [the] *Pesach* [sacrifice], *matzah,* and *maror.* Rather, it was through the performance of these *mitzvos* that the Jews merited redemption. Thus do we respond to the wicked son: '*It is because of this* [זֶה] *[that HASHEM acted on my behalf when I left Egypt.'* זֶה, *this,* refers to the *Pesach* sacrifice, *matzah,* and *maror.*

Following the response to the wicked son, the Torah states: וְשָׁמַרְתָּ אֶת הַחֻקָּה הַזֹּאת לְמוֹעֲדָהּ מִיָּמִים יָמִימָה, *And you shall observe this ordinance* [חק] *at its appointed time from year to year* (*Exodus* 13:10). In essence, every *mitzvah* is a חק, *chok,* for its depth remains unfathomable. The Torah's words are eternal, and each *mitzvah* must forever be observed *at its appointed time from year to year* (*Beis HaLevi*).[2]

---

1. See *Rashi* to *Genesis* 19:3.
2. *Beis HaLevi*, citing the *Midrash,* adds that in the Messianic era, the reasons for such *mitzvos* as *parah adumah* (the red heifer) will be revealed and all the commandments will be understood in greater depth.

The Ten Plagues

◆§ The Ten Plagues occupy a central place in the redemption from Egypt and, as such, are a central theme of the *Haggadah*. In addition to listing the plagues, the *Haggadah* cites Rabbi Yehudah's grouping of them by their initials, and a Tannaic dispute regarding the variant facets of each plague.

The *Midrash* and commentators are replete with explanations of what the plagues represented both individually and as a systematic progression of retribution and revelation. The *Arizal* said the following:

The Mishnah (*Avos* 5:1) states that the world was created with ten utterances. As the Talmud (*Megillah* 21a) explains, the word וַיֹּאמֶר, *and He said*, appears nine times in the chapter of Creation, and the term בְּרֵאשִׁית, *In the beginning*, which introduces the creation of heaven and earth, also represents an utterance.

As mentioned above, the wonders through which God revealed Himself at the Exodus serve as eternal testimony to His being Creator of all that exists. The Ten Plagues correspond to the ten utterances of creation. With each successive utterance, God's Presence became more concealed through the guise of nature. With each successive plague, however, His Presence became more revealed. Therefore, the plagues correspond to the utterances in reverse order. The tenth plague, *the slaying of the firstborn*, corresponds to בְּרֵאשִׁית, *In the beginning*, and the ninth plague, *darkness*, corresponds to וַיֹּאמֶר אֱלֹהִים יְהִי אוֹר, *And God said, 'let there be light'* (*Genesis* 1:3).

The *Zohar* teaches that each Plague was a source of affliction to the Egyptians and a source of healing to the Jews. The Torah relates that while the Egyptians were afflicted with a tangible darkness,[1] *to all the Children of Israel there was light in their dwellings* (*Exodus* 10:23). The Kabbalists write that this light was the אוֹר הַגָּנוּז, the primeval light which God created on the first day and then stored away for the righteous to enjoy in the World to Come.

---

1. *HASHEM said to Moses: 'Stretch forth your hand toward the heavens, and there shall be darkness upon the land of Egypt, and the darkness will be tangible'. . . . there was a thick darkness throughout the land of Egypt for a three-day period. No man could see his brother, nor could anyone rise from his place. . . . (Exodus 10:21-23).*

King David said, *Light is sown for the righteous, and for the upright of heart, gladness (Psalms 97:11).* Spiritual light fills the heart of the upright with a gladness that no earthly pleasure can possibly achieve. Only the upright, who are in touch with their own spiritual essence, can derive pleasure and gladness from a light that is spiritual. To one whose life's goals are the attainment of physical pleasures, spiritual light is actually a source of darkness.[1] The very same light that illuminated the dwellings of the Jews was the source of tangible darkness which left the Egyptians frozen in their places (*Emunas Itecha*).

The Tenth Plague, *the slaying of the firstborn,* was the moment of גָּלוּי שְׁכִינָה, *revelation of the Divine Presence.* The Jews had been mired in the forty-ninth level of spiritual impurity, but their essential spiritual core remained intact. Through the fulfillment of the commandments of circumcision, the Pesach sacrifice, *matzah* and *maror*, they were granted new spiritual life. When God, in all His glory, descended into their midst at the time of the Tenth Plague, the Children of Israel became infused with an awesome sanctity (*HaDei'ah V'HaDibur*).

It was precisely at that moment that they became sanctified as God's Chosen People. It was then that the purpose of Creation — *For the sake of Israel which is called רֵאשִׁית, primary*[2] — was realized.

It was also at that moment that רֵאשִׁית שֶׁבְּרֵאשִׁית, the firstborn offspring of God's choicest flock, attained their own sanctity. However, for the Egyptians, who were essentially impure, the revelation of God's Presence meant death and their firstborn perished (*Ohr Gedalyahu*).

אַרְבַּע כּוֹסוֹת / The Four Cups

Stages of Redemption

◆§ A number of reasons are given for the Rabbinic *mitzvah* of drinking four cups of wine at the *Seder*. The most commonly known reason is that they correspond to the four expressions of redemption used by

---

1. The *Chasam Sofer* once said: "People think that there is a place called *Gan Eden* (Garden of Eden) and a place called *Gehinnom* (Purgatory). And I say that the very same place that is a *Gan Eden* to the righteous is a *Gehinnom* to the wicked."

2. *Rashi* to Genesis 1:1. See p. 38.

God with regard to the redemption from Egypt: וְהוֹצֵאתִי, I will bring you out; וְהִצַּלְתִּי, I will rescue you; וְגָאַלְתִּי, I will redeem you; וְלָקַחְתִּי; I will take [you to Myself as a nation] (Exodus 6:6-7; see Yerushalmi 10:1 and Sh'mos Rabbah 6:4).

Maharal (Gevuros Hashem) elaborates on the significance of these different expressions, and explains that they correspond to the different types of bondage foretold to Abraham at the Covenant Between the Parts [בְּרִית בֵּין הַבְּתָרִים]. There, God revealed to Abraham, 'Your offspring shall be aliens in a land not their own, they will serve them, and they will oppress them. . .' (Genesis 15:13). This prophecy foretells a loss of independence, a state of slavery, and a degree of oppression beyond anything associated with mere slavery.

When the time for redemption arrived, these facets of the bondage were removed in the reverse order of their severity. First, the excessive oppression and tyranny were mitigated — וְהוֹצֵאתִי — I will take you out from under the burdens [i.e. sufferings] of Egypt (Exodus 6:6). Then the bonds of slavery were loosened entirely: וְהִצַּלְתִּי — I shall rescue you from their service. Later, the Jews were granted total independence and departed the land: וְגָאַלְתִּי — I shall redeem you with an outstretched arm and with great judgments.

The goal of redemption was for Israel to become eternally and indelibly identified as God's Chosen Nation — a Nation of Torah. Thus: וְלָקַחְתִּי — I shall take you to Me for a people.

For each of these levels of redemption we thank and praise God with a litany of blessing and song, and drink a cup of wine in gratitude. It should be stressed that each of the Four Cups must be accompanied by its appropriate recitation: the first by Kiddush; the second by Haggadah; the third by Bircas HaMazon; and the fourth by the remainder of Hallel. One who drinks the cups in rapid succession has not fulfilled his obligation (Shulchan Aruch 472:2).

Various other symbolisms are attributed to the Four Cups. They correspond to:

The four times the term כּוֹס, cup, is mentioned in Pharaoh's recitation of his dream, and Joseph's subsequent interpretation of it (Genesis 40: 11,13). This event was one of the occurrences leading to the bondage and ultimate redemption (Meiri).

The four kingdoms destined to rule the world as revealed to Daniel (Daniel 2:31-43, ch. 7-8).

The four "cups of wrath" that will, in the future, be "poured" upon the evildoers of the world. These cups are mentioned in Scripture four times (Jeremiah 25:15, 51:7; and Psalms 75:9, 11:6). Corresponding to these four cups are "four cups of consolation" that God will offer His people at the time of the Future Redemption.

Sign of Freedom

◄§ The abundance of wine drunk at the Seder signifies the theme of חֵרוּת, freedom, which is dominant throughout this night. This concept has halachic ramifications. The Talmud (Pesachim 108b) states that the beverage used for the Four Cups should have the "taste" of wine. Rashbam explains "taste" as referring to wine's power to intoxicate. Accordingly, wine is preferable over grape juice for this mitzvah. The Sages (ibid.) further state that in Talmudic times, when wine was commonly drunk with abundant dilution (because of its strength), one who drank undiluted wine for the Four Cups did not demonstrate freedom in his performance of this mitzvah. Thus, we see that to demonstrate חֵרוּת, freedom, one must discharge his obligation in the preferred manner (in Talmudic times, with diluted wine). R' Moshe Feinstein was therefore of the opinion that one who uses grape juice for the Four Cups has likewise not demonstrated freedom (though he has discharged his obligation. See The Kol Dodi Haggadah by R' David Feinstein).

The Way of Angels

◄§ The intoxicating power of wine dulls the mind. The abundance of wine drunk at the Seder symbolizes the subjugation of our thought process to the will of the One Above (Shem MiShmuel).[1]

As mentioned above,[2] on the Seder night we are akin to Heavenly angels. An angel, by its very nature, can do nothing more than carry out God's will. The very word מַלְאָךְ, angel, means, literally, agent. An agent has no independent power. His legal status is determined solely by the fact that he acts on behalf of his employer. If that sanction is withdrawn, then his actions are invalid. An angel, too, is no more than an agent of its Creator.

Man, however, has independent existence, for he was granted free will to choose between right and wrong. On the Seder night, we drink an abundance of wine to symbolize our desire to rise above the level of angels and dedicate our will solely toward the service of God.

1. Needless to say, one should select a wine that will not prevent him from completing the Seder and fulfilling its many mitzvos.
2. P. 51.

Matzah

Fulfilling the Mitzvah

☙ In detailing the laws of the Pesach sacrifice, the Torah states:

וְאָכְלוּ אֶת הַבָּשָׂר בַּלַּיְלָה הַזֶּה, צְלִי אֵשׁ וּמַצּוֹת עַל מְרוֹרִים יֹאכְלֻהוּ.

And they shall eat the meat on that night, roasted over the fire, and matzos, with bitter herbs shall they eat it (*Exodus* 12:8).

A later verse states: בָּעֶרֶב תֹּאכְלוּ מַצֹּת, *[. . .on the fourteenth day of the month] in the evening you shall eat matzos* (ibid. v. 18). From the fact that the Torah repeats the command to eat *matzah* without making mention of the Pesach meat, the Sages derive that the Scriptural *mitzvah* to eat *matzah* on the *Seder* night is not contingent on the eating of the Pesach meat together with it. Thus, even today with the absence of the Pesach offering, this commandment remains a Scriptural obligation.

A verse in *Deuteronomy* (16:3) juxtaposes the prohibition against eating *chametz* with the commandment to eat *matzah*. This teaches that one can fulfill the *mitzvah* to eat *matzah* only with ingredients which can reach a state of leavening. Thus, the *matzah* used at the *Seder* must be made from the חֲמֵשֶׁת מִינֵי דָגָן, *five species of grain*. They are: wheat, barley, spelt, rye and oats[1] (*Mishnah Pesachim* 2:5). *Matzah* made from rice, for example, would be unacceptable for use on the *Seder* night.[2]

Egg Matzah

☙ The Torah refers to the *matzah* as לֶחֶם עֹנִי, *bread of affliction* (*Deuteronomy* 16:3). This indicates that the *matzah* used to fulfill the *mitzvah* on the *Seder* night cannot be of rich quality. *Matzah* made with eggs or fruit juice, referred to by the Sages as מַצָּה עֲשִׁירָה, *rich matzah*, is unacceptable (*Shulchan Aruch* 462:1).

---

1. In recent years, oat *matzah* has been manufactured in Scotland (under rabbinical supervision) for those who have difficulty eating wheat *matzah*.
2. It is the custom of Ashkenazic Jews not to eat rice on Pesach (as well as any other food that falls under the category of *kitniyos*. See *Rama* 453:1 with *Mishnah Berurah*).

The problem with egg *matzah* (or other forms of מַצָּה עֲשִׁירָה) is not limited to the *Seder*. Some commentators are of the opinion that fruit juice or eggs mixed with flour can result in leavening at a faster pace than flour mixed with water. Others hold that leavening cannot occur unless at least a little water is present in the mixture. However, they *are* concerned that a bit of water may inadvertently become mixed into a batter of flour and eggs (or juice), resulting in an accelerated leavening process. Therefore, says *Rama* (462:4), egg *matzah* or other forms of מַצָּה עֲשִׁירָה should not be used at all on Pesach except by the ill or the aged. Where necessary, one should consult a halachic authority.[1]

"Shemurah Matzah"

◆§ Anyone who has ever visited a Pesach hand-*matzah* bakery recalls the sight of women rolling out their dough as they exclaim: "לְשֵׁם מַצּוֹת מִצְוָה!", "For the sake of matzos mitzvah!" The following is the source for this practice:

The Torah states: וּשְׁמַרְתֶּם אֶת הַמַּצּוֹת, *And you shall guard the matzos* (*Exodus* 12:17). The Sages (*Pesachim* 38b) derive from this that to fulfill the *mitzvah* of *matzah* on the *Seder* night, it is not sufficient that the *matzah* be *chametz*-free. Rather, it is necessary that during the process of its production, the *matzah* had been guarded against becoming *chametz* for the sake of the *mitzvah* to eat *matzah* [לְשֵׁם מַצּוֹת מִצְוָה]. Such *matzah* is known as *matzah shemurah*, *matzah* that was guarded, or colloquially, *shemurah matzah*.

The point in the production process from which such guarding must take place is a matter of dispute among the commentators. *Shulchan Aruch* (453:4) states that it is preferable that the grain be guarded מִשְׁעַת קְצִירָה, *from the time of reaping* and on.[2]

Food of Faith

◆§ *Zohar* refers to the *matzah* as מֵיכְלָא דִּמְהֵימְנוּתָא, *food of faith*. This can be understood in light of *Sefer HaChinuch*'s principle that הָאָדָם נִפְעָל כְּפִי פְּעוּלוֹתָיו, *man is molded by his actions*. The *matzah* symbolizes

---

1. Even in extenuating circumstances, one cannot use egg *matzah* to discharge his obligation to eat *matzah* on the *Seder* night since, as mentioned above, it is not in the category of לֶחֶם עֹנִי.

2. This requirement applies only to the *matzah* eaten on the *Seder* night. However, the Chofetz Chaim notes that the Vilna *Gaon* ate only *matzah shemurah* throughout the festival (*Be'ur Halachah* ד"ה טוב לשמרן). Many follow this practice today.

the faith of the Jewish people, who departed Egypt for the Wilderness without preparing proper provisions for themselves. Therefore, eating *matzah* on the *Seder* night infuses us with faith.

There is another aspect to *Zohar's* description of the *matzah*. During their forty-year sojourn in the Wilderness, the Jews' nourishment came from the manna, the miraculous sustenance which fell from Heaven each day. Our ancestors' dependence on the manna was an exercise in faith and trust in God. This lesson was meant for future generations as well. *And He fed you manna that neither you nor your fathers had known — to teach you that man does not survive by bread alone; rather, through the word of God does man live (Deuteronomy 8:3).*

The Talmud states:

> *And the Children of Israel ate the manna for forty years (Exodus 16:35).* Now, did they actually eat the manna for forty years? Did they not eat it only for forty years minus thirty days?[1] Rather, [the verse teaches that] they tasted the flavor of manna in the cakes [of *matzah*] that they brought out of Egypt[2] (*Kiddushin* 38a).

Thus, the *matzah* represents the manna, a true *food of faith*.

Scripture describes the manna as לֶחֶם אַבִּירִים, *food of angels [lit. of the powerful]* (*Psalms* 78:25). Aside from sustaining the Jews physically, the manna was spiritual food in a very real sense — and so is the *matzah* that we eat on the *Seder* night.

Food for Thought

&§ Most years, the weekly Torah portion immediately following Pesach is *Parashas Shemini*. A main topic discussed in this portion is the *kashrus* laws. After delineating these laws, the Torah stresses that through observance of *kashrus,* a Jew pulls himself up the ladder of holiness; however, by ignoring them, he contaminates his soul and gradually builds a barrier that blocks out his comprehension of holiness.

The eating of *matzah* at the *Seder* serves as an introduction to this concept. Just as eating the *matzah* infuses a Jew with faith, so, too, does the food which a Jew consumes throughout the year have

---

1. See *Rashi* to *Kiddushin* 38a.
2. Thus, they experienced the taste of manna for a full forty years.

a profound impact on his soul's sensitivity to matters of Jewish belief
(R' Yitzchok Kirzner).

Guard the Mitzvos

ఴ To the words וּשְׁמַרְתֶּם אֶת הַמַּצוֹת, *And you shall guard the matzos,*
Rashi cites *Mechilta*:

> Rabbi Yoshiah said: Do not read the word מַצוֹת, *matzos.*
> Rather, read it [as if it were written] מִצְוֹת, *[And you shall
> guard the] mitzvos.* Just as one does not allow the *matzah* to
> become *'chametz'*, so, too, should he not allow a *mitzvah* to
> become *'chametz'* [i.e. delayed] — if a *mitzvah* comes your
> way, do it immediately.

The lesson of *matzah* as applied to general *mitzvah* performance
goes further than the importance of acting promptly. The production
of *matzos* which are guaranteed to be *chametz*-free requires
meticulousness in every detail of the process. Indolence or careless-
ness in one small detail can result in the dough having to be
discarded. Moreover, as explained above, *matzos* used on the *Seder*
night must be produced for the sake of the *mitzvah*.

Similarly, each detail of any *mitzvah* should be accorded proper
attention and the *mitzvah* should be done not for honor or any other
ulterior motive, but purely *lesheim Shamayim* (for the sake of
Heaven).

The Chofetz Chaim (*Zechor L'Miriam*) offered the following
parable:

A king needed hundreds of edifices constructed in his capital city.
An announcement went forth calling on all loyal citizens to come and
offer their time and skills for this project. Many heeded the call.
Instructions were issued for the exact construction of each edifice.
The king underscored two priorities: the workers should pay
attention to detail to ensure that each structure be as beautiful as
possible, and the king's name should be engraved over the entrance
to each building.

In the months that followed, the king was too preoccupied to
check on the progress of the construction. Finally, the day came
when the king embarked on a grand tour of the construction sites.
He was utterly dismayed by what he saw.

Many of the sites were bare; construction had not even begun. Of
those structures that were complete, a large number were products

of shoddy workmanship. Some buildings did, indeed, meet with the king's satisfaction, but for one detail. Over the entrances, alongside the king's name, was engraved the name of someone else!

Said the Chofetz Chaim: One should not be content with performing certain *mitzvos* while neglecting others. A Jew's first concern should be that *all* the King's edifices, i.e., the *mitzvos*, be performed. Next, one should pay careful attention to the details of each *mitzvah* so that the finished product not be one of "shoddy workmanship." Finally, one should strive to perform each *mitzvah* purely to carry out the will of God.

Maror

The Requirement Today

ও§ In contrast to *matzah*, the eating of *maror* (bitter herbs) on the *Seder* night is mentioned only in connection with the consumption of the meat of the Pesach offering: *And they shall eat the meat on that night, roasted over the fire, and matzah, with bitter herbs shall they eat it (Exodus* 12:8). Thus, today, when in absence of the Temple there is no Pesach sacrifice, the eating of *maror* is a Rabbinic ordinance.

This has important halachic ramifications. As with *matzah*, the minimum amount of *maror* that must be eaten is a *kezayis*, a volume equal to the size of an olive. Some hold a *kezayis* to be equal to the volume of one-half an average egg, while others hold it to be equal to one-third an average egg. There is also disagreement as to how our eggs compare in size to those of Talmudic times. For Scriptural *mitzvos* such as *matzah*, we follow the stringent opinion, while for Rabbinic *mitzvos* such as *maror*, one may, in case of necessity, rely on the lenient opinion (*Mishnah Berurah* 486:1).

What to Use

ও§ The Mishnah *(Pesachim* 2:6) lists five types of vegetables that can be used to fulfill the *mitzvah* of *maror*. It is commonly accepted that the first type listed, *chazeres*, is romaine lettuce. The commentators identify the third type, *tamcha*, as horseradish. Some hold that the second type, *ulshin*, is endives. There is no firm tradition regarding the remaining two species.

The most preferred type is *chazeres* (*Shulchan Aruch, Orach Chaim* 473:5). Initially, *chazeres* is sweet, but the longer it remains in the ground, the more bitter it becomes. This recalls the nature of the Egyptian servitude, which was bearable at first, but became progressively worse as time went on (*Mishnah Berurah* §42).

As *Mishnah Berurah* notes, small insects which are not easily discernible are often present on romaine lettuce. To consume even one insect can involve numerous Scriptural prohibitions. Therefore, romaine lettuce should not be used unless each leaf is carefully checked by a God-fearing person. Some use only romaine lettuce stalks which are usually less infested and are more easily checked.[1]

Symbolisms

Maror — Why do we eat this bitter herb? Because the Egyptians embittered the lives of our fathers in Egypt, as it says (Exodus: 1:14): They embittered their lives with hard labor, with mortar and bricks, and with all manner of labor in the field: whatever service they made them perform was with hard labor.

(Haggadah)

Matzah symbolizes the haste with which the Jews were redeemed. *Maror* symbolizes the bitterness of the bondage. Why, then, do we first eat *matzah* and then *maror* on the *Seder* night? Should not the bondage be recalled before the redemption?

When Jacob prepared to leave the Land of Israel for Egypt, God appeared to him and said: *'Have no fear of descending to Egypt . . . I shall descend with you to Egypt and I shall also surely bring you up'* (*Genesis* 46:3-4). This teaches that when the Israelites descended to Egypt, the Divine Presence descended along with them (see *Ramban* ad loc.). And so it was with all subsequent exiles. "Wherever Israel was exiled, the Divine Presence was exiled with them" (*Megillah* 29a). Exile is a time of *hester panim*, Divine concealment, when God hides Himself, as it were. To the non-believer, it may seem as if He is not there, but the man of faith knows the truth . . . *Behold! He was standing behind our wall, observing through the windows, peering*

---

1. For more on the subject, see *The Kol Dodi Haggadah*.

through the lattices (Song of Songs 2:9). God is with us in exile, orchestrating matters in a way that, ultimately, will produce nothing but good for the Jewish people and the individual Jew. *As a man instructs his son, HASHEM, your God, instructs you (Deuteronomy* 8:5).

Maror is bitter tasting. The Chofetz Chaim would often say that a Jew in trouble should never describe his situation as 'bad,' but rather as 'bitter.' Medicine, too, is bitter-tasting, but nevertheless serves a beneficial purpose.[1]

When the Jews departed Egypt, they clearly perceived how the sufferings and persecutions of their exile had been for their good. God had been with them through every bitter moment, as He brought them through the purifying process that would result in their becoming a *kingdom of priests and a holy nation (Exodus* 19:6).

This is why we eat the *Maror,* symbol of exile, after the *matzah,* symbol of redemption. It was after the redemption that the Jews recognized the curative nature of the exile and they gave thanks for it as well.

And so it will be at the time of the Final Redemption. Then, the veils of history will be lifted; we will comprehend all that transpired and perceive that it was all for the good. (The above was based primarily on *S'fas Emes* as elucidated in *Ohr Gedalyahu*.)

The above sheds light on the *Haggadah* passage which derives from a Scriptural source that the *mitzvah* to recount the details of the Exodus can be fulfilled only "when *matzah* and *maror* lie before you." An essential aspect of this *mitzvah* is *hakaras hatov,* to express gratitude to the One Above for all that He has done for us from the

---

1. The Chofetz Chaim once illustrated this thought with a parable:

A traveler who was unfamiliar with the goings-on of the average synagogue stepped into one. He was appalled at the seemingly haphazard system for calling people to the Torah. The first man selected was sitting on the last bench; the second was a gentleman sitting two rows from the front; the third was seated adjacent to the *bimah.* . .

"Excuse me," the man said to the *gabbai* when services had ended, "but wouldn't it make sense to use a more organized system? It is really quite unfair and even insulting to call up people from all corners of the room, leaving other congregants to wonder why they were overlooked!"

The *gabbai* could not help but laugh at the man's ignorance. "You don't understand — I *do* have an organized system. I have a file, with a card for every member of the congregation. On it, I record when each man is *required* to be called to the Torah (as on a *yahrtzeit*). I also record the dates when he was called up during the past few months.

"Of course, to a newcomer like yourself, there seems to be no pattern at all."

We enter the stage of history during a particular scene, said the Chofetz Chaim. Can we expect to understand the Divine reasoning for all that occurs?

time of our Nation's inception[1]. The *matzah* and *maror* that lie before us symbolize that our gratitude must be all-encompassing — for both the good and the bitter alike *(R' Yitzchok Kirzner)*.

Malady Turned Remedy

◄§ Soon after the Exodus, God promised His people:

> *If you hearken diligently to the voice of HASHEM, your God, and do what is just in His eyes, give ear to His commandments and observe all His decrees, then I will not bring upon you any of the diseases that I brought upon Egypt, for I am HASHEM, your Healer (Exodus 15:26).*

Healing is needed when some sort of malady is present. If God promised not to afflict His people with the diseases brought upon Egypt, why then does He refer to Himself as their "Healer"?

The *maror's* symbolism, as explained above, provides the answer. The punishments visited upon Egypt were afflictions in the fullest sense because they did not inspire the Egyptians toward change. In the end, they perished at the Sea, defying the word of God to the end.

In the above verse, God assures His people that if they will hearken to His word and realize the true purpose of life, then whatever future suffering they might endure will in no way resemble the diseases of Egypt. Rather, they will perceive that their pain is part of a healing process, one that ends in heightened purity and a renewed closenesss with their Father in Heaven (based on the thoughts of *R' Simchah Zissel of Kelm*).

A Fitting Conclusion

◄§ The *Haggadah* concludes with the *Chad Gadya* (One Kid) song. In light of the above, this song, as explained by the Vilna *Gaon*,[2] is a fitting conclusion to the *Seder*. Allegorically, the song encapsulates

---

1. Many people have the custom on the *Seder* night to express gratitude for the Divine kindnesses shown to them personally or to their ancestors. In the preface to one of his works, Rabbi Moshe Stern (Debreciner *Rav*) writes: "On the night of סִפּוּר יְצִיאַת מִצְרַיִם, after reciting עֲבָדִים הָיִינוּ, it is my custom to mention and relate that which I lived through and which I saw at Bergen-Belsen. . ."
2. See ArtScroll *Vilna Gaon Haggadah*.

Jewish history, from the sale of Joseph by his brothers and the Jews' subsequent enslavement in Egypt, to the ultimate arrival of the Messiah when the forces of evil, as represented by the angel of Edom, will be destroyed. Thus, we conclude the *Seder* with a declaration that there is a definite pattern to our history, that it is God and God alone Who orchestrates it, and that the long process of wanderings and travail will one day end with all of mankind recognizing and accepting God's sovereignty.

Afikoman

A Lingering Taste

◆§ The Mishnah *(Pesachim* 10:8 and cited in the *Haggadah)* states: אֵין מַפְטִירִין אַחַר הַפֶּסַח אֲפִיקוֹמָן, *One may not eat dessert after the final taste of the Pesach offering.* In the Talmudic era, it was customary that after a meal was completed, various refreshments and delicacies were brought to the participants, much like the dessert of modern times. Those desserts were known as *afikoman.* The Talmud *(Pesachim* 119b) cites the view of Shmuel that just as one does not eat a dessert *[afikoman]* after eating the Pesach offering, so, too, in the absence of the offering, one does not conclude the *Seder* with dessert. Thus, the Sages ordained that the *Seder* meal conclude with the final portion of *matzah* which therefore came to be called *afikoman,* "dessert." The reason for the restriction not to eat dessert is so that "the taste of the Pesach and the *matzah* remain in his mouth"[1] *(Tosafos* to *Pesachim* 120a and *Rambam*, *Hilchos Chametz U'Matzah* 8:9).

This, however, raises a question: Why does the Mishnah say only that dessert cannot be eaten after the Pesach meat, while making no mention of the *matzah*? The Talmud explains that the Pesach offering is mentioned because of its novelty. The insubstantial taste of *matzah* is easily obliterated when eating something else after it. The strong, pungent taste of roast meat, however, does not easily fade and one might have thought that eating dessert after it would be permissible. Therefore, the Mishnah stresses that *even* after the Pesach meat, one may not conclude with dessert.

---

1. Other reasons for this restriction are found in *Talmud Yerushalmi* *(Pesachim* 10:8) and *Rashbam* *(Pesachim* 119b).

Some *(Ramban, Meiri, Ba'al HaMa'or)* are of the opinion that the *afikoman* is eaten in commemoration of the Pesach offering, while others *(Rashi, Rashbam* and *Tosafos)* hold that it corresponds to the *matzah* that was eaten along with the Pesach meat. It should be noted that *Rashi* and *Rashbam* seem to hold that one fulfills his primary obligation to eat *matzah* on the *Seder* night with the eating of the *afikoman.* [1]

Bach *(Tur Orach Chaim* 471) and *Maharil* (cited by *Magen Avraham* 471:1) combine the above approaches. They rule that one should eat the volume of *two kezeisim* (olives) for *afikoman* to commemorate both the Pesach offering and the *matzah* that was eaten with it.

Snatching[2] the Afikoman

⋘ One of the most popular features of the *Seder* is the snatching of the *afikoman* by the children (and their hiding it) after the middle *matzah* had been broken *('Yachatz')* and the portion to be used for the *afikoman* had been carefully wrapped and placed under the pillow of the head of the house.[3]

The Talmud *(Pesachim* 109a) states: רַבִּי אֱלִיעֶזֶר אוֹמֵר: חוֹטְפִין מַצּוֹת בְּלֵילֵי פְסָחִים בִּשְׁבִיל תִּינוֹקוֹת שֶׁלֹּא יִשְׁנוּ. The term חוֹטְפִין indicates an action done with quickness and can be interpreted alternatively as: *we hurry, we grab hold of* or *we snatch.* According to the first interpretation, Rabbi Eliezer teaches that *we hurry to eat the matzah on the night of Pesach for the sake of the children, so that they do not fall asleep (Rashi).* According to the second interpretation, Rabbi Eliezer teaches that *we grab hold [and lift up] the matzah on the night of Pesach for the sake of the children, so that they [be stimulated to ask questions and] do not fall asleep (Rashi* in an alternate interpretation).

Rambam (Hilchos Chametz U'Matzah 7:3) writes:

---

1. See *Sha'ar HaTziyun* 477:4.

2. Rabbi Shimon Schwab notes that it is forbidden to steal as a "joke," with the intention of returning the object afterwards (see *Rambam, Hilchos Geneivah* 1:2). To refer to the *Afikoman* custom as "stealing the *Afikoman*" is contrary to proper *chinuch.*

3. *Mishnah Berurah* (473:58) cautions that the *afikoman* should not be wrapped in cloths that were washed with wheat derivatives (which was common in his time). Likewise, the material should be free of cornstarch and other *kitniyos* derivatives (see *Rama* 453:1 with *Mishnah Berurah*).

Children should be cautioned against hiding the *afikoman* where there is dirt or where *chametz* items are stored.

We must do things differently on this night so that the children will take note and ask, "Why is this night different from all other nights?" Then we will answer them, "This and this is what transpired . . ."

And how do we do things differently? We distribute to them candies and nuts, we remove the table from in front of them before they have eaten,[1] *we snatch the matzah out of the hand,* and other such devices.

Rambam, thus, seems to interpret Rabbi Eliezer's teaching to mean: *we snatch the matzah on the night of Pesach for the sake of the children, so that they [be stimulated by this unusual practice and] do not fall asleep.*

This interpretation may be the source of the custom to have the children snatch the *afikoman* (*Chok Yaakov* 472:2).

A Living Altar

 ◄§ In *Song of Songs* (4:16), God declares: *Awake* [עוּרִי] *from the north and come from the south*, to which the Sages expound: "Let the nation which slaughters its sacrifices in the northern side of the Temple Courtyard be churned [תִּתְנָעֵר], and let the nation which slaughters in the southern side come forth" (*Zevachim* 116a). The *olah* sacrifice, which was entirely burned upon the Temple altar, could be slaughtered only in the northern area of the Courtyard, while sacrifices of which the owner could partake could be slaughtered in other areas as well. In the above verse, the nations of "the northern side" are the gentile nations, whose Temple offerings had to be entirely burned as an *olah*.

From the beginning of time, every sacrifice offered by man was entirely burned as an offering unto God. The first time in history that man partook of sacrificial meat was when the Jews ate of the Pesach sacrifice the night they left Egypt.[2] Having been elevated to the status of God's Chosen People, the Jews' souls had now become an altar of sorts. Thus was every Jew, man and woman alike, required to eat of the Pesach sacrifice.[3]

---

1. In those days, a small table was placed before each person participating in a meal. Today, the *matzah* is covered as a prelude to the asking of the Four Questions.

2. See p. 41.

3. In discussing the attribute of *kedushah*, sanctity, *Mesilas Yesharim* (ch. 26) writes: "When a person becomes sanctified through the sanctity of his Creator, then even his physical acts become matters of sanctity — literally. Illustrative of this is the consumption

In our days, the *afikoman* is symbolic of the portion of Pesach meat consumed by each Jew. When eating the *afikoman,* one should reflect upon the message inherent in it: At the time of the Exodus, God "chose us from among all nations, found favor in us, exalted us and sanctified us with His commandments"[1] (*R' Avigdor Miller*).

"Tzafun"

◆§ In the order of the *Seder* rituals, the eating of the *afikoman* is called *Tzafun,* Hidden. In its plain meaning, this title indicates that the *afikoman* had been safely hidden away so that it could be eaten at this point in the meal *(Sefer HaToda'ah).*

The medieval commentator *Rokeach* suggests that the custom for the head of the house to place the *afikoman* under his pillow is alluded to in the verse, מָה רַב טוּבְךָ אֲשֶׁר צָפַנְתָּ לִירֵאֶיךָ, *How abundant is Your goodness which You have hidden away for those who fear You* (*Psalms* 31:20). This refers to the reward "hidden away" for the God-fearing in the World to Come.

Common custom is for the children who have hidden the *Afikoman* to "strike a deal" with the head of the house, returning the portion of *matzah* in exchange for a promise of gifts. It would seem that this practice is nothing more than another means by which to excite the children so that they will remain awake for as long as possible.

Rabbi Shimon Schwab, quoting his father, sees deep significance in this custom. Earlier in the *Seder,* the middle *matzah* had been broken into two. The smaller portion remained on the *Seder* table as לֶחֶם עוֹנִי, *bread of affliction*, while the larger portion, the *afikoman*, was hidden away. The smaller portion alludes to this world, while the *afikoman* represents the World to Come. The pleasures of this world, though easily accessible, pale by comparison to the spiritual rewards of the World to Come. Those rewards, however, are not free. One must "pay a price," that is, earn them, through observance of Torah and *mitzvos* during his lifetime on this world.

※　※　※

In the Mishnah (*Avos* 2:1) we read, "Be as scrupulous in performing a 'minor' *mitzvah* as in a 'major' *mitzvah*, for you do not know the reward given for *mitzvos.*" Some interpret the phrase, *you do not*

---

of Temple sacrifices, which is a positive commandment and of which the Sages state: "The *Kohanim* eat and [through their eating] the owners gain atonement."

1. From the *Shemoneh Esrei* of *Yom Tov.*

know, as *you cannot comprehend;* i.e. one cannot comprehend the reward for even the smallest good deed. As *Rambam* emphasizes (*Mishnah Sanhedrin* 11:1), in this finite, material world, we cannot conceive of the infinite spiritual rewards stored in the Hereafter. Just as the blind man has no conception of colors, similarly, we have no way of sensing such spiritual bliss as long as our souls are enclosed in their earthly bodies.

As we have seen,[1] the *matzah* alludes to the totality of *mitzvos*. It also represents the faith with which our ancestors followed God *in the Wilderness in a land that was not sown* (*Jeremiah* 2:2). The *afikoman* alludes to the infinite value of every *mitzvah* and of the unwavering faith that connects one to God and permits him to bask in His splendor. It is this "taste" that the Sages wanted us to retain in our mouths, not only on this night, but all year long as well. Thus, we are not permitted to eat anything after the *afikoman.*

In some communities, there is a custom to save a small piece of the *afikoman* as a *segulah*, auspicious omen, for protection against harm throughout the year. *S'fas Emes* relates this custom to the *Seder* night's being a *Leil Shimurim*, Night of Protection. By saving a piece of the *afikoman*, one is symbolically taking the aura of this night with him into the days and months ahead.

S'fas Emes also relates this custom to the verse which teaches that we must recall the Exodus verbally every day of our lives. The Torah states: *... for seven days you are to eat matzos, bread of affliction, for you departed from Egypt in haste — so that you remember the day of your departure from Egypt all the days of your life* (*Deuteronomy* 16:3). Homiletically, this indicates that through the *matzos* [i.e. by saving the *matzah* of *afikoman*], one will recall the Exodus throughout the year.

In discussing the laws of *afikoman,* the Chofetz Chaim cites the words of *Shelah*: "I have seen men of spiritual striving kiss the *matzah* and *maror,* and also the *succah* when they enter and exit it [on Succos], as well as the Four Species [on Succos]. This is to show חִבּוּב מִצְוָה, *love for the mitzvah.* Praiseworthy is he who serves God with joy" (*Mishnah Berurah* 477:5).

---

1. See p. 69.

Hallel

Symphony of Praise

◈§ Hallel (Psalms 113-118) on the Seder night is a Rabbinic obligation. This requirement is based on the verse (Isaiah 30:29): הַשִּׁיר יִהְיֶה לָכֶם כְּלֵיל הִתְקַדֶּשׁ חָג, The song [celebrating Sancherib's downfall] will be for you like [Hallel on the] night of the holiday's sanctification (Pesachim 95b).

Along with the standard Hallel, we recite Psalm 136, which is known as Hallel HaGadol, the Great Hallel, because it underscores God's most enduring achievement — the sustenance of every living thing (Pesachim 118a). The standard Hallel surpasses Hallel HaGadol because its themes are essential articles of Jewish faith. They include: the Exodus; the Splitting of the Sea; the Revelation at Mount Sinai; the Resurrection of the Dead; and the Advent of the Messiah.

Also recited on this night is the beautiful Nishmas prayer which follows The Song at the Sea in the morning prayers on the Sabbath and Festivals. This prayer depicts our utter dependency on God's mercy, our inadequacy to laud Him properly, and our deep resolve to dedicate ourselves to His service. The Talmud refers to Nishmas as Bircas HaShir (the Blessing of the Song) because it continues the theme of the Song at the Sea.

On this night, the Hallel is divided, the first two paragraphs being recited before the meal and the remainder after the meal. The first two paragraphs refer to the Exodus, while the remainder alludes to the future Redemption, which is the theme of the second half of the Seder. By eating the festival meal (Shulchan Oreich) in between the two recitations, we accentuate the fact that this meal, more than any other, is sanctified as a service unto God[1] (Netziv).

R' Mordechai Gifter writes:

> The Seder meal sandwiched in between the Haggadah and the Hallel is truly an act of Divine service. The spiritual elevation of the Jew imparts a different taste to the food. It was Rabbi Yehudah the Prince who once told the Roman

---

1. Shelah writes that during the meal one should discuss the Exodus, sing zemiros, and avoid idle conversation.

Emperor Antoninus that the Sabbath was the special spice which gave a unique taste to the Sabbath meal. The *Seder* service is the special spice of the *Seder* repast. Therefore, parents should take the trouble of maintaining the level of spiritual beauty during the meal. Pesach songs are in order. Torah thoughts — discussing various phases of the *Haggadah* — are of greatest importance. The participation of the child is always to be remembered *(Torah Perspectives)*.

A Song of Freedom

The Mishnah *(Megillah* 20b) states that *Hallel* is recited only by day. *R' Hai Gaon* (cited by *Ran* to *Pesachim* 118a) explains that this applies only to קְרִיאַת הַהַלֵּל, *recitation of Hallel,* whereas *Hallel* on the *Seder* night is in the category of שִׁירָה, *song.*

Turei Even (Megillah 14a) writes that *Hallel* on the *Seder* night is a natural extension of the *mitzvah* to recount the details of the Exodus. This is evident from the text of the Mishnah (which appears in the *Haggadah*): *In every generation, it is one's duty to regard himself as if he personally had gone out of Egypt . . . Therefore, we are obliged to give thanks, to praise, to extol . . .*

Additionally, as a time which is a semblance of the future, when *the righteous will sit with crowns on their heads, enjoying the reflection of God's majesty,* [1] the *Seder* night's aura grants it the status of day.

An allusion to the recitation of *Hallel* on this night is found in the verse, לֵיל שִׁמֻּרִים הוּא לַה' לְהוֹצִיאָם מֵאֶרֶץ מִצְרָיִם, *It is a night of anticipation for HASHEM to take them out of Egypt (Exodus* 12:42). The initial letters of הוּא לַה' לְהוֹצִיאָם form the word הַלֵּל, *Hallel (Rabbeinu Ephraim).*

Below, we present a number of *Hallel* insights which relate to the Exodus and the *Seder* night.

---

1. See Page 48.

From Rags to Riches

מְקִימִי מֵעָפָר דָּל, מֵאַשְׁפֹּת יָרִים אֶבְיוֹן.
He raises the needy from the dust,
from the trash heaps He lifts the destitute
(Psalms 113:7).

⇜ אֶבְיוֹן, *the destitute,* is the poorest of the poor, one who has nothing and, as such, is in need of anything and everything (see *Rashi* to *Deuteronomy* 15:4). In a deeper sense, the term alludes to one who is spiritually impoverished and, in his poverty, craves for every physical want. There is hope even for such a person, for God assures us, "Open for Me an opening like the eye of a needle and I will open for you an opening like that of a huge hallway."

God stands ready to raise each Jew from his or her personal spiritual failures. We need only allow Him entry into our hearts (based on *S'fas Emes*).

The Waters Take Flight

הַיָּם רָאָה וַיָּנֹס
The sea saw and fled (Psalms 114:3).
What did the waters see? The coffin of Joseph.
(Midrash Tehillim)

⇜ The Torah relates (*Genesis* ch. 39) how the wife of Potiphar, whose servant Joseph was, attempted to induce him to sin with her. Day after day he rejected her coaxings, until he was finally forced to flee and, ultimately, suffer imprisonment. Joseph's great inner struggle during the trying period in Potiphar's house is vividly depicted in the Talmud and *Midrash*. He withstood all temptation and rightfully earned distinction as יוֹסֵף הַצַּדִּיק, *Joseph the righteous.* Thus, the sea "fled" in merit of he who *fled and ran outside (Genesis* 39:12).

In fact, Joseph's deed left its imprint upon the entire Jewish nation and this undoubtedly was a factor in the miracle of the Splitting of the Sea.

The Egyptians were a people steeped in immorality. The descendants of Jacob were to live among this sinful nation for more than two hundred years — as slaves for much of this period — and retain their purity all the while. So incredible was this accomplishment that God deemed it necessary to testify to the chastity of the tribes during the bondage. He proclaimed, " I will lend My Holy Name, יָ-ה, to the Jews and add the letters of My Name to their names as testimony to their purity and sanctity." Therefore the tribes are designated הָראוּבֵנִי, הַשִּׁמְעוֹנִי, the *Reuvenites, the Shimonites* (Numbers 26:5-51); i.e., their names are preceded and followed by the letters of Hashem's Name (see *Rashi,* ibid. and *Rashi* to *Psalms* 122:4).

The *Midrash* states: "Because the Jewish nation safeguarded itself against immorality in Egypt, therefore it was redeemed from there." Whence did the nation draw such spiritual strength? "Joseph descended to Egypt and safeguarded himself from immorality; in his merit, all [Jewish] men were safeguarded" (*Vayikra Rabbah* 32).[1]

When the sea saw the coffin of Joseph before it, it saw the collective merit of a people that had remained holy and pure in a land of lowliness and immorality. In the face of such spiritual strength, it had no recourse but to flee.

☙ ☙ ☙

R' Yaakov Kamenetsky *(Emes L'Yaakov)* explains the Sea's flight based on another *Midrash.* At the time of the Exodus, the ministering angel of Egypt declared, "These [the Egyptians] are idol worshipers and those [the Jews] are idol worshipers!" God responded by bringing forth Joseph's coffin. When Joseph was faced with the test involving the wife of Potiphar he was but a lad of seventeen, alone in a strange and sinful land. Aside from the test of natural desire, Joseph was faced with a great inner challenge. He knew that were he to resist the woman's coaxings and flee his master's house, Potiphar's wife would surely slander him in order to conceal the truth of what had occurred. This, Joseph understood, would probably result in his execution or lifetime imprisonment. In fact, Joseph was imprisoned, and were it not for his ability to interpret Pharaoh's Divinely inspired dreams, he would have remained a prisoner there. Joseph's flight from his master's house was *mesiras nefesh* (self-sacrifice) in a most classic sense.

The *Midrash* (*Bereishis Rabbah* 87:6) relates that a gentile matron asked the Talmudic sage R' Yose: "Could it really be that Joseph, a seventeen-year old youth in all his passion, rejected the enticements

---

1. This, says *Zechusa D'Avraham,* is reflected in the verse, *"And all the souls who emerged from Jacob's loins were seventy souls, with Joseph who was in Egypt"* (Exodus 1:5). Those seventy souls were the progenitors of the entire Jewish people. They and all their offspring born during the bondage were all of "the loins of Jacob," conceived in unquestionable sanctity and holiness. How was this possible? *Joseph . . . was in Egypt.*

of that woman?" The gentile psyche simply cannot comprehend such spiritual strength, for it is, indeed, beyond them. Only a Jewish soul, the progeny of Abraham, Isaac and Jacob who themselves withstood many a test, could have acted as Joseph did.

This, essentially, is what Joseph's coffin represented. True, "these and those worshiped idols." However, the Egyptians and the Children of Israel were two intrinsically different peoples. The Egyptians were a lustful and hedonistic lot; their idol worship pointed to their sinful nature. The Jews, on the other hand, were essentially pure and holy; their idol worship was a product of their bondage in a land of sin.

The Nations Give Praise

הַלְלוּ אֶת ה' כָּל גּוֹיִם שַׁבְּחוּהוּ כָּל הָאֻמִּים. כִּי גָבַר עָלֵינוּ חַסְדּוֹ וֶאֱמֶת ה'
לְעוֹלָם הַלְלוּיָהּ.

Praise HASHEM, all you peoples; laud Him, all you nations! For His kindness to us was overwhelming, and the truth of HASHEM is eternal. Praise God! (Psalms 117)

◆§ Once, a Russian prince asked R' Yitzchak (*Reb Itzaleh*) of Volozhin to explain why the Psalmist exhorts *non*-Jews, instead of Jews, to praise God for His kindness to Israel. R' Yitzchak replied without hesitation, "You princes plan countless anti-Semitic schemes with which to destroy us, but our Merciful God always manages to foil your plots. Your secret councils are so well guarded that we Jews don't even realize all the ways in which you intended to harm us, nor how God saved us. Only you gentiles see clearly how God's *kindness to us was overwhelming;* therefore only you can praise Him adequately!" (*Iyun Tefillah;* see *Chiddushei HaGriz HaLevi, Exodus* 18:10).

Illustrative of the above is a legend surrounding the birth of R' Yehudah Loeve of Prague, the *Maharal*:

The *Maharal's* mother was seated at the *Seder* table when she began experiencing the pangs of childbirth. Meanwhile, a gentile was heading toward her home carrying a sack which contained a corpse. This was during the era when the infamous "blood libels" were often used to stir up the populace against the innocent Jews. The gentile planned to deposit the corpse somewhere on the property of the *Maharal's* father R' Bezalel, a leader of his community.

Suddenly, the *Maharal's* mother screamed. Some of R' Bezalel's guests ran out of the house to call the midwife. By now, the gentile had almost reached the house. He had heard the scream. When he saw the people running from the house, shouting in a language which he did not understand, he was sure that he had been discovered. He turned and fled in a panic — and was spotted by a guard who stood watch over the Jewish ghetto. The gentile was caught and the Jews were saved from disaster.

From Revulsion to Reverence

אֶבֶן מָאֲסוּ הַבּוֹנִים הָיְתָה לְרֹאשׁ פִּנָּה.

The stone which the builders despised has become the cornerstone!   (*Psalms* 118:22)

◆§ Israel is called אֶבֶן, *stone* (*Genesis* 49:24), for Israel is the cornerstone of God's design for the world. The world endures only by virtue of Israel's observance of God's laws, a fact which has influenced all nations to appreciate and accept certain aspects of Hashem's commands. If not for the order and meaning which Israel has brought to the entire world, the world would long ago have sunk into chaos.

Ironically, the nations of the world never appreciated Israel's essential role in their survival. The *builders,* i.e. the rulers of the nations, despised the Jews; they demanded that the Jews be expelled or annihilated, claiming that they were parasites who made no contribution to the common good.

But when the dawn of redemption arrives, all nations will realize that Israel is the *cornerstone* of the world (*Radak*).

סְפִירַת הָעוֹמֶר / Counting the Omer

Count of Anticipation

You shall count for yourselves — from the morrow of the rest day, from the day when you bring the Omer waving — seven weeks, they shall be complete. Until the morrow of the seventh week you shall count, fifty days; and you shall offer a new meal offering to HASHEM (*Leviticus* 23:15-16).

When the Temple stood, there was a *mitzvah* to offer a communal meal-offering on the sixteenth of Nissan, the second day of Pesach.

The measurement of coarsely ground barley flour used was an *omer,* a volume equal to 43.2 eggs. On the day the offering was brought, a forty-nine-day count was begun, culminating with the Festival of Shavuos on the fiftieth day.

Today, in the absence of the Temple and the *Omer*-offering, the commentators disagree as to whether the *mitzvah* of *Sefiras HaOmer* (Counting the *Omer*) is Scriptural or Rabbinic.

In discussing this *mitzvah, Sefer HaChinuch* writes:

> The whole foundation of Israel is Torah and it is because of Torah that heaven and earth were created, as it is written, *If not for My covenant [that is to be studied] day and night, I would not have put forth the orders of heaven and earth* (*Jeremiah* 33:25). The purpose for which Israel was redeemed from Egypt was to receive the Torah at Sinai and uphold it . . . This [the receiving of the Torah] was of greater significance to them than their having gone from bondage to freedom.
>
> Therefore . . . we are commanded to count the days from the morrow of the first day of Pesach until the day when the Torah was given, to demonstrate our great desire toward this exalted day for which our hearts yearn, much like a slave who craves for relief and forever keeps count of the days until the moment of freedom for which he longs. For when a person keeps count [until a certain day arrives] he demonstrates that his whole desire and longing is to reach that day.
>
> We reckon our count from the day on which the *Omer*-offering was brought, counting how many days have passed, rather than how many days are left [until Shavuos]. This method shows our powerful desire to reach that day; we do not want to begin our count by mentioning the many [i.e. forty-nine] days it will take until the day of Shavuos has arrived . . .
>
> [The *Omer*-offering was the first Temple offering brought from the new crop.] We associate the counting with the *Omer* for it [the *Omer*] is a noteworthy offering. It alludes to our faith in God's Providence, and that in His desire to sustain mankind, He provides us with a new crop year after year.

Season of Soul-Searching

◄§ In the prayer which many communities recite after the *Omer* counting, we find that the *Sefirah* period is a time of soul-searching:

> *Master of the Universe, You commanded us through Moses, Your servant, to count the Omer count in order to cleanse us from our encrustations of evil and from our contaminations . . . .*

Such spiritual cleansing has its roots in the seven-week period that bridged the Exodus with the giving of the Torah. As already mentioned, Israel had been corrupted by the sinful environment of Egypt and had fallen to the forty-ninth level of spiritual impurity. The *mitzvos* of circumcision and the Pesach sacrifice earned the Jews sufficient merit to be granted the great gift of גִּלוּי שְׁכִינָה, *revelation of the Divine Presence,* on the night of the Exodus. This revelation was, essentially, a gift from Heaven [אִתְעָרוּתָא דִלְעֵלָּא, *an awakening initiated from Above*], to rescue the Jews from the morass into which they had sunk. The next day, with the Divine Presence having ascended to its Heavenly abode, the Jews were left with the task of making themselves worthy [אִתְעָרוּתָא דִלְתַתָּא, *an awakening initiated from below*] to receive the Torah by scaling forty-nine levels of purity, one per day. The revelation which they had been privileged to experience left them markedly changed in two respects: They now felt a tremendous yearning to attach themselves to the One Above; and they now perceived their own spiritual failings and were ready to embark on the path of repentance with zeal and determination.

The Torah refers to the day on which the *Sefirah* count begins as מִמָּחֳרַת הַשַּׁבָּת, *on the morrow of the Sabbath,* that is, the morrow of the first day of Pesach. The use of the word שַׁבָּת, *Sabbath,* to represent the first day of Pesach stirred up much controversy in Talmudic times. The heretical Baitusim sect sought to interpret the words *morrow of the Sabbath* as referring to Sunday. According to them, Shavuos would always fall on a Sunday. The Sages succeeded in proving the Baitusim wrong (*Taanis* 17b). The question remains, however: Why did the Torah use the term *Sabbath* here, thereby leaving its meaning open to question?

Our above discussion serves as one answer. The term שַׁבָּת, *Sabbath,* alludes to the essence of the first night of Pesach, a semblance of the יוֹם שֶׁכֻּלּוֹ שַׁבָּת, *Day of Everlasting Sabbath,* when "the righteous will sit with crowns upon their heads enjoying God's majesty." It was the Divine revelation of that night which inspired the soul-searching of the seven weeks that followed. And it is the aura of the *Seder* night which, to this day, should inspire a Jew to utilize the days of *Sefirah* as a preparation for the Festival of Shavuos (*HaDei'ah V'Hadibur*).

Comparative Counts

◄§ *Zohar* likens the seven-week *Omer* count to the seven clean days which a *niddah* (menstruant) must count before she can immerse herself in a *mikveh.* [1] Although a *niddah* counts seven *days,* Israel needed to count seven *weeks* because of the degree of their contamination. Only after this extended period of soul-cleansing could they unite with God and His Torah at Sinai.

The first night of Shavuos, in particular, is dedicated to this holy union. It is therefore distinguished by the custom of remaining awake to study Torah throughout the night. The *niddah*'s immersion in the *mikveh* is represented by our immersion in the waters of Torah (*The Call of the Torah*).

There is, however, a basic distinction between these two counts. Though the Torah states וְסָפְרָה לָהּ, *and she shall count* (*Leviticus* 15:28), the *niddah* is not required (according to the accepted opinion)[2] to *verbally* count the seven clean days. With the *Omer* count, however, the *mitzvah* can only be fulfilled through verbal counting.

The reason for this distinction lies in the nature of the respective counts. The seven clean days of the *niddah* do not, of themselves, purify. Rather, they serve as a precondition to immersion in the *mikveh* which purifies. With the *Omer* count, however, the *count itself* — if utilized properly — brings about spiritual cleansing. The nightly count should inspire us to take note of the days of *Sefirah* that have passed and of the days that still remain. One should ask himself: "How have I spent the days of *Sefirah* thus far? Have I begun to search my soul and strive to improve? What remains to be accomplished in the days ahead?" Such reflection is a primary purpose of the *Omer* count and is a key in the cleansing process. Therefore, the Torah required that the days of *Sefirah* be counted verbally (*HaDei'ah V'Hadibur*).

---

1. See *Niddah* 66a and *Shulchan Aruch, Yoreh Deah* 183:1.
2. See *Chochmas Adam* 117:14.

Chol HaMoed

Days of Sanctity

⊷§ The Festivals of Pesach and Succos both begin and end with holy days during which work is forbidden. The intermediate days of each Festival are known as חוֹל הַמּוֹעֵד, *Chol HaMoed*, or חוֹלוֹ שֶׁל מוֹעֵד, *Cholo shel Moed* [lit. *the mundane part of the Festival*].[1] The name *Chol HaMoed* alludes to the fact that, unlike the beginning and concluding days which have a degree of holiness so great that nearly all forms of labor are forbidden, the intermediate days are relatively חוֹל, *mundane,* in that many forms of work are permitted.

Rambam (*Hilchos Yom Tov* 7:1) writes:

> Though the term שַׁבָּתוֹן, *rest day,* is not associated with *Chol HaMoed*, the term מִקְרָא קוֹדֶשׁ, *holy convocation,* is; additionally, it [*Chol HaMoed*] was a time when the *Chagigah* [Festival] offering could be brought during the Temple era. Therefore, it is a time when [certain forms of] labor are prohibited so that it not be like a regular weekday which has no sanctity at all.

The Talmud (*Moed Katan* 18a) cites a Scriptural verse as the source for prohibition of labor on *Chol HaMoed*. *Rambam* (along with *Tosafos*, *Rosh* and others) hold that this verse is used as an אַסְמַכְתָּא, a Scriptural text in support of a Rabbinic law. However, other early commentators disagree. They (*Rashi, Rashbam, Rif* and others) hold that these labors are Scripturally prohibited. However, there is a very basic distinction between the laws of forbidden labor on *Chol HaMoed* and all other Scriptural prohibitions. Here, the Torah authorized the Sages to determine which forms of work to permit and which to prohibit.[2]

---

1. In *Eretz Yisrael*, only the first and last days of the Festival are full holy days — *Chol HaMoed* thus consists of the second through the sixth day of Pesach and the second through the seventh day of Succos. In the Diaspora, however, since we celebrate the first *two* and the last *two* days of each Festival with a full degree of holiness, *Chol HaMoed* is the third through the sixth day of Pesach and the third through the seventh day of Succos.

2. The laws of *Chol HaMoed* form the core of Tractate *Moed Kattan* [lit. *Minor Festival*] and are detailed in *Shulchan Aruch* ch. 530-549. For an excellent contemporary

As *Rambam* makes clear, the days of *Chol HaMoed* are *not* weekdays. They are חול, *mundane*, only by comparison to the other Festival days in which almost all forms of labor are prohibited. *Zohar* (*Shir HaShirim*) speaks of the sanctity of *Chol HaMoed* as a reflection of the Festival days which precede and follow it.

The Sages (*Avos* 3:15) speak harshly of הַמְבַזֶּה אֶת הַמּוֹעֲדוֹת, *one who disgraces the Festivals.* In his commentary, *Rabbeinu Yonah* explains:

> The term used here is מְבַזֶּה, *disgraces,* rather than מְחַלֵּל, *desecrates,* for the Mishnah here speaks not of *Yom Tov*, which is akin to the Sabbath. Rather, it speaks of one who performs a forbidden labor on *Chol HaMoed.* In doing so, he disgraces *Chol HaMoed*, for he is essentially saying, "These days do not have the sanctity of the first days [of *Yom Tov*]; therefore, we can do any sort of labor!" He has done something despicable, without any shame.

In discussing the laws of *Chol HaMoed*, the Chofetz Chaim cites the words of *Kolbo*: "God's intention in granting us the Festivals is so that we cling to Him in awe and love and toil in His Torah" (*Mishnah Berurah* 530:2).

The Chofetz Chaim also writes that one's manner of dress on *Chol HaMoed* should reflect the sanctity of these days, though one is not required to wear Sabbath or *Yom Tov* finery.[1] He notes, however, that *Maharil* would wear his Sabbath caftan on *Chol HaMoed* (*Mishnah Berurah* 530:1).

Time of Joy

◆§ The Torah states: וְשָׂמַחְתָּ בְּחַגֶּךָ, *You are to rejoice on your Festival* (*Deuteronomy* 16:14). From here the Sages derive: "One is obligated to be joyous and happy of heart on the Festivals, together with his wife, children and everyone else who is with him" (*Shulchan Aruch* 529:2; see *Mishnah Succah* 4:1 and *Pesachim* 109a). *Chol HaMoed* is included in this *mitzvah*. One should, therefore, eat meat and drink wine on each day of *Chol HaMoed* (*Be'ur Halachah* 529 s.v. כיצד משמחן). In contrast to *Yom Tov*, one is not obligated to have bread

---

treatment of these laws, see *Chol HaMoed K'Hilchaso* (Hebrew) by Rabbi Yekusiel Farkas (Jerusalem, 1987) and *Chol HaMoed* (English) by Rabbi Dovid Zucker and Rabbi Moshe Francis (New York, 1981).

1. *Magen Avraham* is of the opinion that one should wear *Yom Tov* finery. See *Sha'ar HaTziyun* 530:4.

with his meal on *Chol HaMoed*. Nevertheless, it is a *mitzvah* to do so both by day and by night (*Mishnah Berurah* 530:1).

The Talmud states:

> *The Holy One, Blessed is He, said to the Jewish People: "My sons, borrow on My account and sanctify the holiness of the day; trust in Me and I will repay your loans."*
>
> *. . . All of a person's income is fixed [for the coming year] between Rosh Hashanah and Yom Kippur with the exception of expenditures for the Sabbaths and Festivals, and the expenditures for teaching one's children Torah. [With regard to these expenses,] if one spends less, he receives less; and if he spends more, he receives more* [1] (*Beitzah* 15b-16a).

Tur (ch. 419 citing *Pesikta*) states that expenditures for *Chol HaMoed* are included in the above. The *Arizal* taught that one who honors the Festivals and spends money to delight in them with food and drink *lesheim Shamayim* (for the sake of Heaven) will be repaid twofold. An allusion to this can be found in the word מוֹעֵד *[Festival]*. The numerical value of the first letter, מ, is forty. The sum total of the remaining letters is 80 (ו = 6; ע = 70; ד = 4). One who spends 40 for the Festivals will be repaid with 80 (*S'dei Chemed*).

Yosef Ometz (§839) writes, "While it is a *mitzvah* to delight in *Chol HaMoed* with food and drink, nevertheless, its sanctity is primarily one in which the soul, not the body, takes pleasure. On these days, one should set aside more than the usual time for Torah study."

שְׁבִיעִי שֶׁל פֶּסַח / The Seventh Day of Pesach

The Splitting of the Sea

◄§ It was on the twenty-second of Nissan, the seventh day of Pesach, that the miracle of the Splitting of the Sea occurred. This miracle was the climax of the wondrous events of the Exodus.

---

1. The amount a person is allotted by Heaven to fund these *mitzvos* is not fixed in advance. Rather, depending on what he spends on these *mitzvos*, the profitability of his ventures is increased or decreased accordingly (*Rashi*).

The Chassidic masters spoke of the awesome sanctity of this day and the potential within it for spiritual rejuvenation. R' Yisrael Alter of Ger finds an allusion to this potential in the Torah. The Song at the Sea is preceded by the phrase וַיּוֹשַׁע ה׳ בַּיּוֹם הַהוּא, *And HASHEM saved on that day [Israel from the hand of Egypt]* (*Exodus* 14:30). The Torah makes specific mention of the salvation having occurred on *that day* to allude to the fact that the twenty-second of Nissan remained a day of spiritual salvation for all generations.

Another allusion can be found in *Song of Songs*, much of which allegorically depicts Israel's relationship with God after the Exodus (see below). Israel pleads to God, ''מָשְׁכֵנִי אַחֲרֶיךָ נָּרוּצָה, *Draw me, we will run after You!''* (*Song of Songs* 1:4). מָשְׁכֵנִי, *Draw me,* alludes to the first night of Pesach, regarding which Israel was commanded: מִשְׁכוּ, *Draw forth. . .[lambs for the Pesach offering]* (*Exodus* 12:21). אַחֲרֶיךָ, *after You,* alludes to the seventh day of Pesach, which Scripturally (and even today for those residing in Israel) is שֶׁל אַחֲרוֹן פֶּסַח, *the last day of Pesach.* Both the first and the seventh days of Pesach are times of spiritual awakening when the Jewish soul can become inspired to exult: נָּרוּצָה, *we will run after You!* (*Beis Yisrael*).

Like the *Seder* night, the essence of this day is אֱמוּנָה, *faith.* The seventh day of Pesach was one on which Israel demonstrated *mesiras nefesh,* self-sacrifice, and faith of the highest order, as will be explained below.

"And They Had Faith in HASHEM"

⋐§ After relating how the Jews had crossed the Sea, the Torah states:

וַיַּרְא יִשְׂרָאֵל אֶת הַיָּד הַגְּדוֹלָה אֲשֶׁר עָשָׂה ה׳ בְּמִצְרַיִם, וַיִּירְאוּ הָעָם אֶת ה׳,
וַיַּאֲמִינוּ בַּה׳ וּבְמֹשֶׁה עַבְדּוֹ.

Israel saw the great hand that HASHEM inflicted upon Egypt; and the people revered HASHEM, and they had faith in HASHEM and in Moses, His servant (*Exodus* 14:31).

Why does the Torah state here, at the Exodus' conclusion, that the Jews had faith in God? Did they not have faith in Him when they departed Egypt after the slaying of the Egyptian firstborn? In fact, the Torah testifies to their faith even *before* the Ten Plagues had begun. After returning to Egypt from Midian, Moses related to the Jews what God had spoken to him, and he also performed certain Divinely ordained signs. There, the Torah states: וַיַּאֲמֵן הָעָם, *And the people had faith* (ibid. 4:31).

Moreover, faith, by definition, is belief in something that is not clearly visible for all to see. What need was there for faith after *Israel saw the great hand that HASHEM inflicted upon Egypt?* The Sages relate that at the Splitting of the Sea, Israel became a nation of prophets and witnessed revelations greater than the esoteric visions of the prophet Ezekiel. The truth of God's existence, omniscience and omnipotence was as clear as day. Could belief at such a time be called "faith"?

The answer to this is that there are infinite levels of *emunah*, faith in God.[1] However, all levels of faith fall under one of three basic categories. There is אֱמוּנָה בְּמוֹחַ, *intellectual faith;* אֱמוּנָה בְּלֵב, *faith in one's heart;* and the highest level, אֱמוּנָה בָּאֵבָרִים, *faith which encompasses one's entire being.* Yesod HaAvodah[2] states that the distance between *intellectual faith* and *faith in one's heart* is greater than the distance between heaven and earth. אֱמוּנָה בָּאֵבָרִים, *faith which encompasses one's entire being,* was the faith of King David who declared, '*All my bones shall say: 'HASHEM, who is like You?' '* (*Psalms* 35:10). This is a faith which allows for no fear of any kind other than the fear of God. It is a faith that proclaims אֵין עוֹד מִלְבַדּוֹ, *there is none beside Him* (*Deuteronomy* 4:35), even in the most terrifying and seemingly hopeless situations.

When God instructed Moses to return to Egypt to lead the Jews and begin the process of redemption, Moses protested, '*But they will not believe me . . .*' (*Exodus* 4:1). God responded that the Jews were *ma'aminim b'nei ma'aminim*, believers, sons of believers (*Shemos Rabbah* 3:12). They were descendants of Abraham, of whom it is written, *And he had faith in HASHEM* (*Genesis* 15:6). They had inherited a faith whose essence could become obscured and dimmed but not extinguished. Moses returned to Egypt and, as God had foretold, *the people had faith.* But this was אֱמוּנָה בְּמוֹחַ, *intellectual faith;* it did not, as of yet, penetrate their hearts.

As the Ten Plagues progressed and the various stages of redemption unfolded, the Jews' faith grew. By the time they departed Egypt on the fifteenth of Nissan, their hearts were permeated with faith in God. Nevertheless, from their reaction upon seeing the approaching Egyptian armies as they headed toward the sea, it is clear that they had not yet attained the highest level of faith: *Pharaoh approached; the Children of Israel raised their eyes and behold!* —

---

1. See p. 29.
2. Citing R' Leib Madokar, a disciple of the *Maggid* of Mezritch.

Egypt was journeying after them, and they were very frightened; the Children of Israel cried out to Hashem (Exodus 14:10).

God's response was that this was not a time for prayer. The Jews now had the opportunity to rise to the highest level of faith. To earn this, they would have to demonstrate unshakable trust in God as they faced a terrifying situation. Hashem said to Moses: 'Why do you cry out to Me? Speak to the Children of Israel and let them go forth!' (ibid. v. 15; see Rashi). The Jews heeded the call. Led by the prince of the Tribe of Judah, Nachshon the son of Aminadav, they entered the sea fearlessly — and it split (Sotah 37a). What was their reward? They had faith in God and in Moses, His servant. They had attained אֱמוּנָה בְּאֵבָרִים, the highest level of faith (Nesivos Shalom).

The Song at the Sea

אָז יָשִׁיר מֹשֶׁה וּבְנֵי יִשְׂרָאֵל אֶת הַשִּׁירָה הַזֹּאת לַה׳. . . .
Then Moses and the Children of Israel sang this song to Hashem . . . (Exodus 15:1).

Moses said before the Holy One, Blessed is He: "I know that I sinned before You with the word אָז, then, as it is written, 'And from the time [וּמֵאָז, lit. and from then] that I came before Pharaoh to speak in Your Name he did evil to this people . . .' (ibid. 5:23). Therefore, I now begin Your praise with the word אָז" (Shemos Rabbah 23:3).

Following Moses' first confrontation with Pharaoh, in which he demanded in the name of God that the Jews be permitted to journey into the Wilderness to offer sacrifices, the persecutions increased. The Jews were required to fulfill their quotas of brickmaking without being supplied the necessary straw as they had been in the past. When the quotas were not met, the Jewish taskmasters were beaten. In their anguish, the taskmasters blamed Moses for their added suffering.

Moses, in turn, asked God, 'Why have You done evil to this people; why have You sent me? From the time that I came before Pharaoh to speak in Your Name he did evil to this people, but You did not rescue Your people.'

The commentators explain Moses' outcry as a result of his having thought that his mission to Pharaoh would at least in some small way signal the beginnings of redemption (Ibn Ezra), or that the process would begin soon after his visit to the royal palace (*Ramban*). Neither, it seemed, had occurred.

Hashem responded,[1] "My ways are not your ways, for I accomplish judgment and compassion simultaneously."

Moses accepted God's response without comprehending how compassion was manifest amid such judgment. As the Exodus reached its climactic end with the Splitting of the Sea, he was able to look back at all that had transpired throughout the exile and perceive that, indeed, all had been for the good. In the most difficult times, God's attribute of compassion was manifest. Therefore, he began his song of praise with the very word with which he had expressed dismay (based on *Ohr Gedalyahu*).

An Abode for His Presence

זֶה אֵלִי וְאַנְוֵהוּ.

This is my God and I will glorify Him (Exodus 15:2).

וְאַנְוֵהוּ — *I will build for Him a sanctuary* [נָוֶה] (*Targum Onkelos*).

וְאַנְוֵהוּ — *I will relate His beauty* [נוֹי] *and praise to all the people of the world* (*Rashi*).

וְאַנְוֵהוּ — *Beautify yourself* [הִתְנָאֶה] *before Him through mitzvos. Make a beautiful succah, a beautiful lulav, a beautiful shofar . . .*(*Shabbos* 133b).

וְאַנְוֵהוּ — *Emulate Him* [אֲנִי וָהוּא, *I and Him*]; *just as He is gracious and merciful, so should you be gracious and merciful* (*ibid.*)

The masters of *mussar* teach that when one experiences a spiritual awakening, he must immediately act upon it, for if not, he runs the risk of being left with nothing more than a fading memory. When the Jews crossed the Sea of Reeds and clearly perceived the Divine Presence in a way that surpassed the visions of the great prophets, they yearned to have God's Presence remain with them permanently. Therefore, they declared, *I will build for Him a sanctuary*, an abode for the Divine Presence.

In truth, every Jew can transform himself into a sanctuary, and this desire, too, was expressed by the Jews in their Song at the Sea. *Nefesh HaChaim* (footnote to 1:4) cites the well-known comment

---

1. As explained by R' Yosef Karo in *Maggid Meisharim*.

to the verse וְעָשׂוּ לִי מִקְדָּשׁ וְשָׁכַנְתִּי בְּתוֹכָם, *And let them make for Me a Sanctuary so that I may dwell among them* (*Exodus* 25:8). The verse does not read, וְשָׁכַנְתִּי בְּתוֹכוֹ, *And I will dwell in it [i.e. in the Sanctuary]*, but וְשָׁכַנְתִּי בְּתוֹכָם, *And I will dwell within **them**; i.e. within each and every one of them. Every Jew must strive to transform himself into a veritable sanctuary. How is this accomplished? *Nefesh HaChaim* explains:

> If man will sanctify himself appropriately through the observance of all the *mitzvos* . . . then he is a Sanctuary — literally — and the Divine Presence rests within him; as it is written, "The sanctuary of Hashem are they" (*Jeremiah* 7:4).

A Jew becomes an abode for the Divine Presence when he sanctifies himself in thought, speech and deed. In thought, he seeks to internalize the attributes of his Creator. *Just as He is gracious and merciful, so should you be gracious and merciful.* In speech, he strives in both tone and content to speak words that proclaim Whom he represents: *I will relate His beauty and praise to all the people of the world.* In deed, he strives to fulfill God's commandments in as beautiful a manner as possible. *Beautify yourself before Him through mitzvos.*

Thus, all four interpretations to the word וְאַנְוֵהוּ are essentially one (*Ohr Gedalyahu*).

The Song's Conclusion

⋙ The Song at the Sea concludes with, ה׳ יִמְלֹךְ לְעֹלָם וָעֶד, *God shall reign for all eternity.* With these words, the Jewish nation prayed that just as God had demonstrated His sovereignty at the Splitting of the Sea when He rescued those who revered Him and destroyed those who scorned His word, so may He do the same in all generations.

The word יִמְלֹךְ (*He shall reign*) is written without the ו, [חָסֵר] to allude to the fact that in reigning over mankind, God is not overbearing. It is a principle of Jewish faith that God never presents an individual with a test that is beyond his capabilities. To quote *Midrash:* "We do not find the full strength of God's power in His dealings with His creations, for God does not make matters overly difficult for them. Rather, He acts toward man in accordance with man's ability" (*Shemos Rabbah* 34:1).

The word יִמְלֹךְ is future tense — *He shall reign.* However, *Targum Onkelos* uses present tense: ה׳ מַלְכוּתֵהּ קָאֵם לְעָלַם וּלְעָלְמֵי עָלְמַיָא,

HASHEM — *His kingdom is established forever and ever*. This may allude to God's transcendence of time; to Him, past, present and future are one (*Rabbeinu Bachya*).

The Song begins with the words יָשִׁיר אָז, which, literally, are translated: *Then [Moses and the Children of Israel]* **will sing**. Rashi comments: "From here the Sages derive a Scriptural allusion to the Resurrection of the Dead [in the future]." *Rabbeinu Bachya* notes that the Song contains eighteen verses, corresponding to the eighteen vertebrae of the spine which will become renewed at the time of the Resurrection and burst forth with song.

The Sages taught: "The eighteen blessings of *Shemoneh Esrei* [the *Amidah*] were ordained to parallel the eighteen verses of the Song at the Sea" (*Midrash Shochar Tov*). As the Talmud relates (*Berachos* 28b), the Sages of Yavneh established the nineteenth blessing [*V'LaMalshinim*] against the heretics who persecuted the Jews and made every attempt to turn them away from God and His Torah. The custom to repeat the verse ה' יִמְלֹךְ לְעֹלָם וָעֶד when reciting the Song in the morning prayers might be to parallel the nineteenth blessing. While the heretics mouth their falsehoods we declare that *God shall reign for all eternity* (*Oznayim LaTorah*).

The Women's Song

וַתִּקַּח מִרְיָם הַנְּבִיאָה אֲחוֹת אַהֲרֹן אֶת הַתֹּף בְּיָדָהּ, וַתֵּצֶאןָ כָל הַנָּשִׁים אַחֲרֶיהָ בְּתֻפִּים וּבִמְחֹלֹת. וַתַּעַן לָהֶם מִרְיָם, שִׁירוּ לַה' כִּי גָאֹה גָּאָה סוּס וְרֹכְבוֹ רָמָה בַיָּם.

Miriam the prophetess, the sister of Aaron, took the drum in her hand and all the women went forth behind her with drums and with dances. Miriam spoke up to them, "Sing to HASHEM for He is exalted above the arrogant, having hurled horse and its rider into the sea" (Exodus 15:20-21).

The Torah refers to Miriam as *the sister of Aaron* because she was a prophetess even before her brother Moses was born. As the Talmud (*Megillah* 14a) relates, she had said, "In the future, my mother will bear a son who will save Israel."

But why must the Torah allude to this fact here?

The Sages relate that in the early years of the bondage, when Pharaoh issued the decree that all Jewish boys be drowned in the river, the men fell into despair. Amram, leader of the generation, separated from his wife. His young daughter Miriam came forth with a convincing argument: "Your decision is worse than Pharaoh's decree! Pharaoh's decree is directed against the newborn males, while yours will ensure that no babies at all be born!" As a result, *A man [Amram] went forth from the house of Levi and took [i.e. retook] a daughter [Yocheved] from Levi* (Exodus 2:1).

Three months after Moses was born, his mother, fearing his discovery, put him into a wicker basket which she placed among the reeds at the riverbank. Amram said to Miriam, "What of your prophecy that this child would be the redeemer?" Miriam did not despair. *His sister stationed herself at a distance to know what would be done with him* (ibid. v. 4).

R' Zalman Sorotzkin makes the following observation: It was unlikely that Jews, fearing the king's wrath, would go along the riverbanks searching for babies who had been cast into the waters. As for the Egyptians, they would almost certainly have overturned the basket so that the baby would drown. How did Yocheved and Miriam expect the child to be saved?

It can only be that Moses' mother was convinced that God would work miracles for the child who, Miriam had prophesied, would save Israel. In addition the young prophetess herself was sure that her prophecy would come true; therefore, she stood off to the side to see what would happen to him. Miriam had no doubt that God would work a miracle, and only wanted to see what sort of miracle it would be (*Oznayim LaTorah*).

And sure enough, a miracle occurred. That very day, Pharaoh's daughter came to the river to "cleanse herself of her father's idolatry" (*Sotah* 12b). Pharaoh's daughter discovered the basket and rescued the child. Miriam came forward and offered to find the baby a Jewish wet nurse — and so it was that Moses was returned to his own mother.

The Talmud states: "In the merit of the righteous women of that generation were our forefathers redeemed from Egypt" (*ibid.* 11a). Miriam, who never lost faith that her prophecy would be realized, epitomized the greatness of the Jewish women of her day. Thus does the Torah allude to that prophecy when the women sang their Song at the Sea.[1]

---

1. The Torah states: וַתַּעַן לָהֶם מִרְיָם, *and Miriam spoke up to them* ['Sing to HASHEM . . .] The term לָהֶם is masculine; it alludes to the strength of the women's faith, which was superior to that of the men (*Shelah*). Their faith is evident from their having prepared drums before they left Egypt to accompany the song which they expected to sing (*Mechilta*).

שִׁיר הַשִּׁירִים / Song of Songs

Song of Eternal Love

≈§ The prophets, in writing of Israel's relationship to God after they have strayed from His path and evoked His wrath, frequently use the analogy of a wife who has betrayed her husband and thereby aroused his anger. Solomon composed *Shir HaShirim* (Song of Songs) in the form of that same allegory. It is a passionate dialogue between the husband [God] who still loves his estranged wife [Israel], and the wife, who longs for her husband and seeks to endear herself to him once more.

The term *Songs of Songs* in its basic interpretation defines this Book as *the ultimate song. Rishon L'Tzion* (by the author of *Ohr HaChaim*) explains the term *Song of Songs* with a parable of a king who became disenchanted with his queen and sent her away. All were certain that the two were separated forever. Their son, however, decided to probe the matter. He spoke privately with his father and discovered that the king *did* long for his queen and was hopeful that there would be a reconciliation. Then the son went to his mother and learned that she, too, yearned for her spouse! In his exultation, the son composed two songs: one described the king's love for the queen and the other, the queen's love for the king.

Shir HaShirim, which portrays the love of God for His people and the love of Israel for God, is a *song composed of two songs*.

Rambam (*Hilchos Teshuvah* 10:3) writes:

> What is proper love [of God]? It is that one love God with an exceedingly great and powerful love until his soul becomes bound up in this love and is forever preoccupied with it . . . as we are commanded, [*And you shall love* HASHEM, *your God,*] *with all your heart and with all your soul* (*Deuteronomy* 6:5). This is what Solomon intended allegorically in writing, . . .*for* [*bereft of Your Presence*] *I am sick with love* (*Song of Songs* 2:5). All of *Shir HaShirim* is an allegory on this theme.

Holiest of Holies

*Rabbi Akiva said: All of the songs [of Scripture] are holy but
Shir HaShirim is holiest of holies (Yalkut Shimoni).*

◆§ It is most appropriate that from among all the Sages, it was Rabbi
Akiva who expressed the loftiness of this song. At the age of forty, he
was an ignorant shepherd who despised Torah scholars. Rachel,
daughter of the wealthy Kalba Savua, perceived the hidden potential
within him. She married Akiva and paid the price of being
disinherited by her family. The new couple lived in abject poverty as
Akiva began to study Torah. Rachel sent her husband off to the
academies of the great Sages of the day, where he studied for twelve
consecutive years without once returning home. When he finally
returned home, he overheard the neighbors ridiculing his wife for
having married a man who was both ignorant and uncaring. She
replied, "He is studying Torah. If only he would spend another twelve
years doing the same!"

Rabbi Akiva fulfilled his wife's wish. Twelve years later, he returned
with twenty-four thousand disciples who thirstily drank every drop of
wisdom that poured forth from his lips. Having learned of his arrival,
Rachel made her way through the throngs that stood around her
now-famous husband. Not knowing who this shabbily dressed
woman was, Rabbi Akiva's disciples sought to have her removed.
Rabbi Akiva told them, "Leave her, for all of my Torah and all of your
Torah belongs to her."

Rabbi Akiva knew better than anyone what selfless devotion is. He
was most qualified to perceive the loftiness of a song that depicts the
selfless love between God and His Chosen Nation, and declare it to
be "holiest of holies" (*R' Avigdor Miller*).

Pesach and the Sabbath

◆§ The Sages interpret much of *Shir HaShirim* as the story of Israel after
the Exodus, a time of such great spiritual passion that God said
centuries later: *I remember for your sake the kindness of your youth,
the love of your bridal days, how you followed Me in the Wilderness
in an unsown land (Jeremiah 2:2)*. It is therefore customary to read
Shir HaShirim privately at the conclusion of the *Seder (Chayei Adam*

130:16) and publicly on the Sabbath of *Chol HaMoed*. [1] When the seventh or last day of Pesach falls on the Sabbath, it is read then (*Rama* 490:9). The Sabbath day is particularly appropriate for the reading of *Shir HaShirim* because it represents the pinnacle of *dveikus* [spiritual attachment]; to the extent that one attaches himself to the Sabbath, he attaches himself to the One Above. [2]

The Torah states: *And on the day of your gladness, on your Festivals, and on your new moons you are to sound the trumpets over your elevation offerings. . .* (*Numbers* 10:10). *Sifri* expounds: וּבְיוֹם שִׂמְחַתְכֶם, *And on the day of your gladness — These are the Sabbaths*. This seems difficult, for the *mitzvah* of שִׂמְחָה, *joy*, is found with regard to the Festivals; nowhere in the Torah is there a command to be joyous on the Sabbath. *Nesivos Shalom* explains that in *Shir HaShirim*, the day of marriage is called יוֹם שִׂמְחַת לִבּוֹ, *the day of his heart's gladness* (3:11). To a bride and groom, their wedding day is one whose essence is joy. Similarly, the Sabbath, as a day of intense attachment to God, is one whose essence is joy.

❀ ❀ ❀

A fundamental relationship between Pesach and the Sabbath is found in the Torah itself. In the first reading of the Ten Commandments (*Exodus* 20:11), the Sabbath is described as a symbol of God's creation of the universe. However, in the second reading, the redemption from Egypt is given as the reason for this *mitzvah*: *And you shall remember that you were a slave in the land of Egypt, and HASHEM your God took you from there with a mighty hand and an outstretched arm. Therefore, HASHEM, your God, commanded you to make this day of the Sabbath* (*Deuteronomy* 5:15).

Ramban (ibid. 5:15) explains that the two concepts are intertwined. The Sabbath *is* symbolic of creation. However, it was the Exodus which demonstrated to humanity that God controls all of nature, directing it as He sees fit. Thus, the events of the Exodus bear witness to that which the Sabbath represents, while the testimony of Sabbath observance brings to mind the Redemption. As *Ramban* puts it, "The Sabbath is a remembrance of the Exodus, while the Exodus is a remembrance of the Sabbath." [3]

---

1. *Mishnah Berurah* (490:18) notes that the *piyutim* recited on the Sabbath of *Chol HaMoed* are patterned after many of the verses in *Song of Songs*.

2. See *Ramban* to *Numbers* 28:2.

3. See ArtScroll *Shabbos* (Holiday series, pp. 44-47 and 137). As mentioned above (p. 86), the Torah refers to the first day of Pesach as שַׁבָּת, *Sabbath*. One reason for this

The Voice of My Beloved

קוֹל דּוֹדִי הִנֵּה זֶה בָּא, מְדַלֵּג עַל הֶהָרִים מְקַפֵּץ עַל הַגְּבָעוֹת.
The voice of my beloved! Behold it came suddenly [to redeem me], as if leaping over mountains, skipping over hills (Song of Songs 2:8).

Rabbi Yehudah said, 'The voice of my beloved' — this is the voice of Moses. When Moses came and said to Israel, "This month you will be redeemed," they said to him, "Moses, how can we be redeemed? Did not God say to Abraham, 'And they shall serve them and they shall afflict them four hundred years' (Genesis 15:13), and so far only two hundred and ten years have passed?"

Moses replied, "Since God desired to redeem you, He disregards your calculations, but 'leaps over the mountains' (i.e. the calculations)."

Rabbi Nechemiah said, ". . . they said to him, 'Moses, how can we be redeemed? We are lacking good deeds!'" Moses replied, "Since He desires to redeem you He disregards your evil deeds — and of whom does He take note? The righteous among you, such as Amram and his court, and their deeds" (Shir HaShirim Rabbah 2:1).

Certainly, the *Midrash* does not mean to imply that God ignored the sins of the Jews in order to bring about their redemption. The Sages explain the command, *Draw forth* (מִשְׁכוּ) *and take for yourselves [Pesach] lambs for all your families* (*Exodus* 12:21), to mean, "Withdraw (מִשְׁכוּ) your hands from idol worship and take for yourselves lambs of *mitzvah*" (Rashi to *Exodus* 12:6 citing *Mechilta*). Surely, the Jews required soul-cleansing from other sins as well.

Rather than ignore their sins, God brought about His people's redemption *despite* their sins. In His kindness, He calculated the four hundred years of exile as beginning with the birth of Isaac. And in merit of the righteous, such as Amram (Moses' father) and his court, God presented the Jews with commandments that would spark their

---

might be because both represent a spiritual awakening initiated from Above [אִתְעָרוּתָא דְלְעֵילָא]. The sanctity of the Sabbath and its impact on one who experiences it in the desired manner are far beyond anything that a person could attain through his own efforts. Thus does God refer to the Sabbath as "a precious gift" hidden away in His treasure house (*Beitzah* 16a).

spiritual revival, culminating with their receiving the Torah seven weeks later at Sinai.

The Jews had not imagined that they could be worthy of redemption at that time. God, however, reckoned differently.

In the Book of *Genesis* (12:16), *Ramban* states the principle: *Everything that happened to the Patriarchs is a portent for their descendants.*

The Chofetz Chaim applied this principle to the passage pertaining to Sarah's disbelief at the foretelling of the birth of a son (ibid. 18:12-15). Sarah had reflected on her withered physical condition and incredulously wondered whether she could bear a child.

Then God said to Abraham, *Why is it that Sarah laughed, saying, 'Shall I in truth bear a child, though I have aged?'* — *Is anything beyond Hashem?*

Why, asks the Chofetz Chaim, does the Torah — in which there is not one unnecessary letter — record at length an incident that is uncomplimentary to the righteous Matriarch?

The Chofetz Chaim explains that this episode is a foreshadowing of the situation that will exist prior to the final redemption:

This episode alludes to *Ikvesa D'Meshicha,* the period that will immediately precede the arrival of the Messiah, when God's glory will be revealed in this world. In the period of *Ikvesa D'Meshicha,* there will surely be great leaders of Israel who will be as the prophets of old and exhort the masses to strengthen their faith and return to God through repentance. They will also arouse the people to prepare themselves for the Messiah's arrival through the study of Torah and the performance of good deeds.

The Torah hints to us here that at that time, there will be men small of faith, who will not believe the words of their reprovers, as we find regarding the Egyptian exile: . . . *but they did not heed Moses, because of shortness of breath and hard work (Exodus 6:9).* Therefore, the Torah hints to us that the Holy One, Blessed is He, will find fault with these people and say, "Is anything beyond Me?"

. . . My friends and brothers: Let us examine the situation in which we find ourselves today. The Jewish people are drowning in a sea of troubles in all parts of the world. The sacred teachings of our holy Torah are cast downward lower and lower from day to day. On all sides, our enemies seek to destroy us . . . The new generation is being reared without Torah or faith and is being taught to deny belief in God and His Torah. If this situation continues much longer, Heaven forfend, who knows where it will bring us?

Logic dictates that the arrival of the Messiah cannot be far off. It is in our hands to hasten our redemption by returning to God in perfect repentance, and by preparing ourselves through Torah study and good deeds.

May Hashem, in His compassion, inspire us and the entire Jewish nation to return to Him in perfect repentance, so that we may merit the Final Redemption, speedily and in our time.

(*Chofetz Chaim al HaTorah* p. 56)

Pesach Stories

Modern-Day Labans

ঙ Go and learn what Laban the Aramean planned to do to our father Jacob; for Pharaoh decreed only against the males but Laban attempted to uproot everything . . . .

(*Haggadah*)

The Brisker *Rav* (R' Yitzchak Zev Soloveitchik) once visited the Chofetz Chaim and found him discussing our people's travails in exile; in particular, the wave of anti-Jewish edicts that were then being promulgated by the Polish government. The Chofetz Chaim related the following:

A ninety-year-old Jew had applied to the Polish government for a passport. When the man told the attending clerk that he did not own a birth certificate, he was told that unless he could produce two witnesses who could attest to where and when he was born, he would not receive a passport. Of course, this was impossible, for anyone who was old enough to recall this man's birth would have been past one hundred years of age!

"Such unfairness!" declared the Chofetz Chaim. "Didn't they realize that there was no way the man could fulfill their demand? What were they trying to prove?"

The Chofetz Chaim explained, "When our forefather Jacob was confronted by his father-in-law Laban after having fled the latter's house, Laban demanded an explanation. Jacob replied by reminding Laban of the schemes to which he had been subjected for the past twenty years. *'I served you fourteen years for your two daughters, and six years for your flocks; and you changed my wage a hundred times'* (Genesis 31:41). What was Laban's reply? *'The daughters are my daughters, the children are my children and the flock is my flock, and all that you see is mine'* (ibid. v. 43).

"What kind of a reply was that? In no way did it respond to the serious charge with which Laban had been confronted! This, however, was typical of Laban. As far as he was concerned, Jacob's claims did not exist. It was as if they had not been uttered. As such, there was no reason to respond to them.

"Claims and counterclaims can only exist when each party recognizes the other as a claimant. Then, the two sides can bring their case to court for a decision. But when one side does not even respect the other as a claimant, the situation cannot be dealt with."

The Chofetz Chaim continued, "Of course it's unfair to ask a ninety-year-old man to bring witnesses for when he was born. But this can be argued only when the claimant is considered a claimant. As far as the Polish government is concerned, however, we Jews are a non-entity. They govern us with a different set of rules and all our arguments are not reckoned with at all.

"So what can we do?" he concluded. "I cannot offer advice that is better than that of Rabbi Eliezer the Great who said, *'What can a person do to escape the "birthpangs of the Messiah" [i.e. the travails that will precede the Final Redemption]? Let him involve himself in the study of Torah and in performing acts of kindness' "* (Sanhedrin 98b).

Bittersweet

Ⱁ R' Nachman of Breslov told the following story:

A Jew and a gentile were traveling together. On the eve of Pesach they found themselves in a town where they did not know a soul. The Jew told the gentile: "Tonight is the holiday of Passover. In every community, special attention is given to ensure that everyone has a proper festive meal. You can come with me to the synagogue and pose as a Jew. I am sure that in no time at all we will both be invited to eat at someone's table." The Jew gave his companion a brief, incomplete description of the *Seder*.

That night, the two went to the synagogue where each was extended a separate invitation. The gentile found himself at the table of a learned Jew, who elaborated for hours on the many wonders of the Exodus. While the Jew's children listened with rapt attention, the gentile squirmed and fidgeted as he waited for the festive meal which, his friend had assured him, would eventually be served.

Finally the moment arrived — or so he thought. The head of the house recited blessings over the *matzah* and distributed portions to the assembled. The gentile would have preferred a thick piece of bread, but he knew better than to voice his feelings. As he chewed the flat wafer, he thought of the chicken soup that Jews were well known for.

How utterly shocked and disappointed he was when, instead of a steaming bowl of soup, he was handed a piece of horseradish! This was more than he could handle. With anger and disgust, he threw the horseradish on the table, muttered something under his breath and stormed out of the house.

The next day, the gentile met his Jewish friend and related his terrible experience. The Jew could not help but laugh. "I forgot to mention the *maror!* Had you been patient for a few more minutes, you would have had the food that you were waiting for."

A Jew lives by his faith, and faith requires patience and self-discipline. Esau lacked these qualities, and so he traded the birthright and accompanying benefits to satisfy his momentary hunger. As we recite in the *Haggadah*, Esau's portion is Mount Seir, not the Land of Israel, which the Children of Israel earned through their experiencing the purifying process of the Egyptian servitude, represented by the *maror*.

Guarded by the Matzos

•§ In pre-War Europe, *matzah shemurah* was very expensive. Most people ate *matzah shemurah* only at the *Seder*, when it is required.[1] Among the minority who ate such *matzah* throughout the Festival was R' Alter Shapiro, a scholarly businessman who resided in Lomza,

---

1. See p. 67.

Poland. When asked why, he explained: "I'm a businessman. In the world of business, there exist all sorts of loopholes to make money; some of them are 'kosher' while others are not. When I am faced with an opportunity for an easy gain through an unjustifiable loophole, I tell myself: 'Alter, a Jew who eats *matzah shemurah* the entire Pesach would consider doing such a thing? *Ach!* Shame on you!' And that is sufficient to hold me back."

(R' Chaim Shapiro in *The Jewish Observer*)

Priorities

◈§ One year, poor health prevented R' Yisrael Salanter from personally supervising the baking of his Pesach *matzos*. As his disciples prepared to leave for the bakery, they asked whether there was anything in particular in which they should be especially stringent. "Yes," R' Yisrael replied. "The woman who kneads the dough is a widow. Be especially careful not to hurt her feelings."

❦ ❦ ❦

R' Shmuel Eliezer Eidels, known as the *Maharsha* (1555-1631), is known for his classic Talmudic commentary, which is found in most editions of the Talmud and is considered basic for in-depth understanding of Talmudic discourse. Aside from his Talmudic genius, the *Maharsha* was exemplary as a man of boundless kindness. It is told that outside his home in Ostroh, Poland, where he served as *rav*, a plaque bore the words of Scripture: בַּחוּץ לֹא יָלִין גֵּר דְּלָתַי לָאֹרַח אֶפְתָּח, *Let no stranger spend the night outside, my door is open to any guest* (Job 31:32).

In advent of Pesach each year, the *Maharsha* would commission the baking of many pounds of *matzos* which he would distribute to the poor. These *matzos* were stored in his home and were kept separate from the *matzos* which were prepared for his personal use. The latter were prepared under his own personal supervision and their baking process incorporated *chumros* (stringencies) not commonly employed.

One *Erev* Pesach, the *Maharsha* went to select the *matzos* that would be placed upon the *Seder* table, but could not find his *matzos*. When he told his wife where he had stored the *matzos* and asked if she might know what had happened to them, she blanched. She had thought that those were the *matzos* designated for the poor and had given them all away. The *Maharsha*, probably for the first time since his youth, would have to make do with *matzos* which, while fit for use, had not been prepared under his personal supervision.

The *Maharsha* reacted by excusing himself and going into another room where he proceeded to pace back and forth. There, he was overheard repeating to himself again and again, מַשֶּׁהוּ חָמֵץ דְּרַבָּנָן, מַשֶּׁהוּ "בַּעַס דְּאוֹרַייתָא, *A minute amount of chametz is Rabbinically forbidden,* [1] *but a minute amount of anger is prohibited by the Torah."*

Help From Above

During Pesach, the Ponovezh *Mashgiach*, R' Yechezkel Levenstein, would frequently exclaim: אַלֶס הָאט דֶער אוֹיבֶּערְשְׁטֶער גֶעטָאהן!, *Everything was accomplished by the One Above!* Once, at the *Seder,* he explained himself:

In the *Haggadah*, we read: *Then I took your father Abraham from beyond the river and led him through all the land of Canaan (Joshua 24:3).* Asked R' Levenstein: Why do we not make mention on this night of Abraham's faith, of his having come to recognize God's existence at a time when the world was steeped in idol worship? Why do we mention only God's "taking" Abraham while omitting our forefather's own spiritual awakening?

At the time of the Exodus, God granted the Jews a Heavenly gift in lifting them from the forty-ninth level of impurity to the loftiest spiritual heights. Pesach, therefore, is a time to recognize that *all* spiritual accomplishments are achieved only with *siyata diShmaya*, Divine assistance. True, Abraham did seek out his Creator while living in a world of heresy, but he could not have accomplished anything without God reaching out toward him. On the *Seder* night, we focus on this aspect of Abraham's achievements. Yes, concluded R' Levenstein, "אַלֶס הָאט דֶער אוֹיבֶּערְשְׁטֶער גֶעטָאהן!"

❧ ❧ ❧

The above concept is illustrated by the following story, told by R' Yekusiel Yehudah Halberstam, the Klausenberger *Rebbe*, שליט"א:

There once lived a *tzaddik* who burned with a passion to serve his Creator. One year, as Pesach approached, he began to ponder the significance of the *mitzvah* to avoid consumption of even the tiniest particle of *chametz*. The *tzaddik* desired to ensure that, this year, his

---

1. According to Scriptural law, a mixture becomes forbidden only if it contains an amount of *chametz* equivalent to the size of a *kezayis* (an olive — see p. 70).

home be rendered *chametz*-free as never before. He decided to involve himself in the pre-Pesach preparations in a way that he had never done, especially with regard to the preparation of the Festival foods.

For weeks he toiled, a true labor of love. He supervised the cleaning, the food purchasing, the baking of the *matzos* and more. Everything went smoothly, just as he had hoped.

The *Seder* night arrived. The *tzaddik* felt an unusual sense of exhilaration. He had worked hard, but it was well worth it. When the time came for *Shulchan Orech*, the festive *Seder* meal, he thought of all the effort that had gone into readying the kitchen in which these foods had been prepared.

Suddenly, the *tzaddik* gasped. There, in his bowl of soup, was a wheat kernel! The unthinkable had occurred. The kernel was considered actual *chametz* and rendered all the soup, the pot in which it had been cooked, and the utensils with which it had been served, unfit.

The *tzaddik* was devastated. Something like this had never before happened to him. How could it possibly have happened when he had been so overly zealous?

Using Kabbalistic methods, the *tzaddik* inquired the following of Heaven: How had it happened and why did it happen? He received the following response: It had happened when a bird flew over his house and dropped the kernel as it passed over his chimney. The kernel fell through the chimney and into the pot of soup which was cooking on the stove directly below it.

The reason why it happened was that the *tzaddik*, though his intentions had been for the sake of Heaven, had omitted one crucial detail. He had neglected to *pray* that his efforts be blessed with success. Because he had relied entirely on his own efforts, he failed.

More than Meets the Eye

ৼ§ When Rabbi Yosef Dov Soloveitchik (author of *Beis HaLevi*) was *Rav* of Slutzk, a blacksmith once came before him with the following question: Can one fulfill the obligation of *Arba Kosos* (the Four Cups) with milk? R' Yosef Dov replied in the negative. He then asked, "Is it perhaps for health reasons that you wish to use milk?" The man replied, "No, I and my family are in good health. I simply cannot afford to buy wine." R' Yosef Dov promptly gave the man twenty-five rubles.

When the man had left, someone asked the *Rav*, "Wine for Pesach costs only a few rubles. Why did you give him so much?"

R' Yosef Dov replied, "If this man was considering using milk for the *Arba Kosos*, then obviously he was not planning on serving meat or chicken at the *Seder*. He needs far more than wine and that is why I gave him twenty-five rubles."[1]

Functions of a Rebbetzin

◆§ Each year in advance of Pesach, Rabbi Yosef Chaim Sonnenfeld, Rabbi of Jerusalem, would distribute to Jerusalem's needy large sums of money which had been sent to him by mail from overseas.

One year, the money did not arrive until *Erev* Pesach shortly before noon. As Jerusalem's *Rav*, R' Yosef Chaim had to remain at home to be available to answer the many Festival-related halachic queries which the city's residents would pose. He therefore turned to his wife and said, "I realize that your preparations for the *Seder* have barely begun, but the poor are desperately in need of the monies which have just arrived. We already have *matzah, maror* and wine — the most basic holiday needs — and we can have a happy *yom tov* with that. However, the poor will not have a happy *yom tov* if they will be deprived of the staples which they are accustomed to purchasing for the festival. Who knows? Such deprivation might even lead to strife and discord in some homes. Please stop what you are doing and deliver these funds to them."

Rebbetzin Sonnenfeld fulfilled her mission, returning home just before the *yom tov* began. That night, happiness reigned in

---

1. *Talmud Yerushalmi* states that each community must provide the poor of their city with money with which to purchase *matzah* for Pesach (see *Rama* 429:1). This money is colloquially known as *ma'os chitim*, money for wheat, because in ancient times families would buy wheat and process it into flour for baking. Of this obligation, the Chofetz Chaim writes: "Perhaps the reason why the Sages enacted the giving of such money for Pesach more than for the other festivals is that Pesach is *z'man cheiruseinu*, the season of our freedom, when we sit reclined [in the way of free men]. At a time when each man and his family are in a state of such joy, it is not an honor for God that the poor be hungry and thirsty. Therefore, we give the poor man a sufficient amount of flour [for *matzah*] for the entire festival of Pesach so that he, too, will be able to relate the story of the Exodus in a spirit of joy.

"Another obvious reason for this enactment is that *chametz* is forbidden during Pesach, and *matzah* is not that easy to come by; if we will not provide for the poor man for all the days of Pesach, he might go hungry or come to stumble [with regard to the festival commandments]. This last reason is cited in *Mateh Yehudah*" (*Sha'ar HaTziyun* 429:10).

Jerusalem, especially in the Sonnenfeld home (from *Guardian of Jerusalem* by R' S.Z. Sonnenfeld).[1]

Meal of Freedom

∾ It was late on the eve of Pesach, 5686 (1926) when Rabbi Yosef Chaim Sonnenfeld heard a knock at his door. Four community leaders from Budapest who had come to Palestine for the holiday were calling on the Holy City's revered leader. R' Yosef Chaim received them warmly. In the ensuing conversation, the visitors expressed a desire to be guests at R' Yosef Chaim's *Seder*. However, they insisted that the *Rav* permit them to pay for the food that they would eat. One of the men immediately placed a large sum on the table. R' Yosef Chaim said that it would be his pleasure to have such honored guests and he accepted the sum that had been offered.

The men were somewhat surprised by R' Yosef Chaim's quick acceptance, for they had been told that their gesture would surely be rejected. The poverty in R' Yosef Chaim's home was well known, but so was his boundless kindness for Jews of all stripes. Moreover, R' Yosef Chaim's poverty was, in part, a result of his absolute refusal to accept assistance of any kind from anyone. It seemed out of character for him to so readily permit his guests to pay for their meal.

The following night the men joined R' Yosef Chaim around his *Seder* table. As one of them later put it, "It was one of the most awesome experiences of my life to see the holy, glowing face of R' Yosef Chaim on the *Seder* night."

During the festival's Intermediate Days, the guests were visited at their hotel by R' Yosef Chaim. After conversing with them, the *Rav* withdrew the *Seder* payment from his pocket and placed it on the table. When asked for an explanation, R' Yosef Chaim replied, "It is really quite simple. Pesach is the Festival of freedom. What kind of freedom is it for a person to feel that he is imposing on someone else? I accepted your payment so that you would feel comfortable in my home and would feel free to eat as much as you wanted. Now that you have enjoyed the *Seder*, I can return your money" (*Guardian of Jerusalem*).

---

1. What makes this story particularly poignant is that the Sonnenfelds themselves lived a life of poverty. R' Yosef Chaim received a meager salary from the Kollel Ungarin which supported Jewish settlement in the Holy land; he absolutely refused any gifts or other monetary benefits to which he was entitled in his position as *Rav* of Jerusalem.

Seder Night in Block 20[1]

At the concentration camp in Mauthausen, Germany, the food situation was impossible. One loaf of bread was rationed for eight men. The daily soup was inedible. I had always managed to eat everything, even in Birkenau, but in spite of gnawing hunger I could not tolerate the Mauthausen soup and vomited from it.

In fact, I *did* have an alternative. On our journey to Mauthausen, the train had lurched to a halt. The door slid open slightly and we saw an open car loaded with wheat kernels standing nearby. Within easy reach were hundreds of kernels. We scooped up several handfuls of the stuff before the train began to move again.

"It's exactly thirty days to Pesach," I had said, breaking the silence. "We ought to save these kernels — Who knows? Maybe we'll be liberated by Pesach, and we will use these for *matzos mitzvah!*"

Now, it was two weeks before Pesach and we were still prisoners. And the hunger was getting worse with each passing day.

I was approached by three of my friends, Mendel Markus and the Rubenstein brothers. They wanted me to ask the *Block Altester* (Senior) and the *Stuben Altester* (Room Senior) for permission to bake *matzos*, since I was on good terms with them. My friends would take care of the time and place, using the washroom late at night so the SS would not find out. The only problem would be to heat the stove sufficiently so the baking could proceed quickly.

I could not share in their excitement. We were isolated slave-laborers in a prison camp, surrounded by SS men on all sides. The Nazis valued our skills, not our lives. I could not see risking our lives further just to bake *matzos*. And then, what about the prisoners who sleep near the stove? Some were only "half-Jews" and "quarter-Jews." We were so crowded that we practically slept in a heap. They would never tolerate the overheated stove. What would we do if an SS officer would make a sudden appearance? And how would we beat the kernels into flour? The plan was simply too fraught with doubt and danger.

We consulted with R' Avigdor Glanzer, a scholar whose words we all respected, and he agreed with me fully. The others, however, were not convinced.

---

1. This story is adapted from an article by Abraham Krakowski which appeared in *The Jewish Observer*, March 1973 and subsequently was published in *A Path Through the Ashes*.

"But still . . ." one of my friends began. "Maybe we could still manage . . ." another one suggested. "After all, the grain — isn't it a sign from Heaven that God wants us to go ahead and bake *matzos*?" "Look here," I insisted, "no one ever *thought* of baking *matzos* until I said it in that boxcar from Sachsenhausen. It was my idea, and now I say forget about it. As for God wanting us to eat *matzos*, His help can come in a flash, anyway. Let's just leave things to Him."

My retort quieted them, but it did not put my mind at ease. That night I slept fitfully. In my dream, my deceased father and I were visiting the *Rebbe* of Radomsk.

We were standing at the Rebbe's table. Next to him stood his son-in-law, Reb Moshe. (The Rebbe and his son-in-law had been killed by the SS in the Warsaw Ghetto in 1942, together with their wives. I had known that already.) The Rebbe asked me, "What are you going to do about davening (praying) with a minyan (quorum)? It is written: דָּבָר וְלֹא חֲצִי דָּבָר, *'A whole thing, and not halfway.' "*

I answered: "If it is at all possible, we see to it that when someone has to say Kaddish on a Yahrzeit (the anniversary of the death of a parent) we get ten people together. We also manage an occasional abbreviated prayer service."

Suddenly, my father was not there anymore. I realized while dreaming that my father was no longer in this world and I began begging the Rebbe to look into our situation, and that he should pray to God to help us. Then I told him the entire story of the grain. I told him about our discussion and my closing retort. I asked him what he thought about the matter. He answered: "I shall tell you. As a matter of principle you are right, but you will remember how your dear father labored to bake matzos. And it is written: וְכֵן תַּעֲשׂוּ לְדוֹרוֹת, *'And thus you shall do for all your generations.' "*

The dream was over.

The next morning I awoke full of hope that we would be freed. The words were echoing in my ears: "Thus you shall do for all your generations . . . all your generations!" There would be more generations!

I could not wait to hear them call, "Everybody out of bed." I ran directly to R' Avigdor Glanzer and all but shouted, "Glanzer, we'll bake *matzos*!"

He stared at me, and asked, "What happened all of a sudden?"

I told him the entire dream and the impression it had made on me. "If that is the case, I have no counsel to offer and I am in agreement," he said, " — and very happy at that."

I went to Markus and the Rubensteins, and also told them the story, and that we would indeed bake *matzos*. I was so convinced that our liberation was at hand that no guns could scare me.

Glanzer, one of the Rubensteins, and I approached Atze, the Block Senior, for permission to bake the *matzos* in the evening after taps. He asked, "Where do you expect to do all that?"

We told him that the preparation would be done in the washroom, but we would like to have the stove in the room well heated so the baking could be handled with speed. We assured him that the whole operation, from beginning to end, would take only a half hour. He went with us to Ernst Gottlieb, the Room Senior. Both realized that we were serious. They agreed, and added, "Think of us, too."

We quickly began the detailed planning on how to accomplish our task. We washed four towels and hung them to dry on the wall surrounding the yard. After they had dried, we wrapped the grain kernels in the towels and took four hammers (we had access to tools) and beat the grain until late in the afternoon. We did this out in the yard. The guards were puzzled by our actions, but they were not permitted to talk to us, nor we to them. But we could hear them asking each other: "What are they doing there?" As the grain became pulverized, we poured it into a piece of paper. After several hours of arm-aching work, we had collected about two hundred grams of flour.

During the course of the day we found a tin can which we heated through to make it *kosher* for Pesach use. By bedtime the stove was piping hot. When the light was turned off, some of those near the stove started to complain that it was too hot for them. Gottlieb raised his voice, "Krakowski is not to be disturbed in his work. Everyone quiet!" That was sufficient to silence the complaints.

We quickly went into the washroom. We prepared the dough in a bowl we had previously heated and cleaned, and whispering, with tears on our cheeks, we sang snatches from *Hallel*. The kneading and rolling took some ten minutes. We had a board for rolling out the dough, but we had to use an empty bottle as a rolling pin. I then stationed myself at the stove, and every minute or so, one of my co-workers brought me a *matzah* from the washroom. The stove was so hot that it took barely two minutes for six *matzos* to be done. I would slide one *matzah* on and take off another.

We stuck to our schedule, and the entire work was finished in less than eighteen minutes! We had baked sixteen *matzos*, each about the size of the palm of my hand. For the first time in years we went to bed happy.

The next morning we began writing down the *Haggadah* and its recounting of the Exodus from Egypt, piecing it together from whatever anyone could remember by heart.

In the evening, our *Seder* began. Again, we slipped into the washroom. The previous evening we were six in the washroom; that night, fifteen. There were more who wanted to join us, but there was not enough room, and then, we were afraid that the SS might hear us. We started reciting the *Haggadah* very quietly. Some of us could not contain ourselves and broke into sobs. As for me, I could not utter a single word.

When I had quieted down a little, I reminded the others not to forget where we were, and to try to be quick. After we recounted the Exodus from Egypt, we washed our hands and ate a piece of *matzah*. I permitted myself to save a piece the size of a fingernail, as a *segulah* (auspicious omen).[1]

At the conclusion of our *Seder*, after the traditional "Next year in Jerusalem," we said in one voice, as if it were part of the text: "If God will only free us now, we will have to make an even greater *Haggadah*."

For Whom the Matzos?

ود It was two weeks before Pesach and there was no *matzah*. The Bluzhever *Rebbe*, R' Yisrael Spira, approached Commandant Hass of the Bergen Belsen death camp, with an audacious request:

"We wish to celebrate our religious holiday by baking *matzah*. We do not ask for extra rations. All we ask is that we be given flour instead of bread and that we be permitted to build a small oven for ourselves. All the work will be done outside of our regular working hours."

The officer said that the request would be forwarded to Berlin. To the amazement of all, the answer was not to execute those who dared to ask, but to grant them the privilege.

During those busy pre-Pesach days, one of the women in the camp went into labor. She was taken to a nearby hospital to give birth. With her, someone smuggled out a letter addressed to Switzerland. The letter described the inhuman conditions in the

---

1. See p. 78.

camp and begged that some way be found to send food packages to prevent starvation. Ordinarily, patients going to hospitals were able to find ways to forward letters, but this one could not. The letter was discovered on her person and sent back to Commandant Hass. He was furious and he was determined to vent his rage on the *Rabbiner* for whom he had just done a favor.

"*Rabbiner* Spira, I was kind enough to let you bake your filthy *matzos* and then you repay me by sending out this ungrateful lying letter!"

The *Rebbe* answered calmly that he knew nothing of the letter and had no hand in dispatching it.

"But you are the *Rabbiner*. Either you know who sent it or you can find out. If you do not inform me within twenty-four hours who is responsible for this letter, I will have you shot."

The Bluzhever *Rebbe* answered, "I repeat that I know nothing of the letter. If I did know or if I find out who is responsible, I will not tell you. Shoot me now if you wish."

Hass turned to leave. Why the notorious murderer did not add one more victim to his list, no one knows. With his jackboot, he smashed the *matzah* oven and went on his way.

Matzos had been baked, however. Now the question was how they should be divided. The preponderant opinion was that they should be given to adults who were required by the Torah to eat *matzah*. Children had no such requirement and therefore should not be permitted to deplete the scarce supply of *matzos*. However, there was a lone voice raised in opposition — the voice of a woman.

In the camp was a widow (later the *Rebbe's* second *Rebbetzin*) who cared for her two sons and two nieces throughout the war. She came from a distinguished family to which she personally added stature. "We must rebuild the Jewish people with our children," she argued. "They are precisely the ones who should receive portions of *matzah* for if we ever escape this *Mitzrayim* (Egypt), they are our future."

Responsibility for children was more than rhetoric to her. In the camp, she learned of someone who had a Bernfeld *Tanach* (Bible) with German translation. She bought it for three pounds of bread—an enormous fortune in the currency of hunger and suffering of those days—so that she could use it to teach the children, as indeed she did for over two years. Eloquent, passionate, persuasive—she carried the day and in a *hora'as sha'ah* (an extraordinary decision) it was decided that the children would be given *matzah*.

On the *Seder* night, the Bluzhever *Rebbe* conducted a *Seder* for the children of the death camp. Instead of living in freedom and learning about slavery and redemption, he taught them, who were living in slavery, of the hope of redemption and freedom. He interpreted the Four Questions to reflect the concentration camp experience. He told them that the word עֲבָדִים, *slaves*, is composed of the initials of דָּוִד בֶּן יִשַׁי עַבְדְּךָ מְשִׁיחֶךָ, *David son of Jesse, Your servant, Your anointed*. He told them that one day they would look back at the bitterest of exile nights as the prelude of a new redemption. Today, those children, who had learned from a *Tanach* bought with bread and eaten *matzos* baked with tears, are leaders in the rebirth of Torah in America, England, and Israel (from a piece by R' Nosson Scherman in *A Path Through the Ashes*).

Guarded Matzah

◄§ According to the slave laws applied to the Jews in the concentration camps, boys and girls over twelve years of age were compelled to do hard labor.

Some five hundred Jewish girls were interned in a labor camp for girls in Upper Silesia. There was one girl in the camp who came from a family of pious *chassidim* and who brought a *siddur* along with her. Her father had given it to her when she was taken away. All the Jewish holidays were recorded in tiny letters on the first page.

The girl guarded that *siddur* like the apple of her eye. In time of great trouble, when the oppression became unbearable, she would read some *Tehillim* (Psalms) from the *siddur* to her girlfriends. She would read those Psalms which spoke about the wicked with special emphasis, foretelling that they will be "like hay blown in the wind," and that "they will be caught in the net which they had put out," and then both she and her friends would feel relieved. More than once, when despair overwhelmed them all, the girl would check the calendar of the holidays in her *siddur*, and then proceed to calculate and find out when the next holiday would be coming. She would then look for some way to celebrate that holiday without getting caught.

One day, the owner of the *siddur* announced that Pesach was only a few days away. "Let's hold a secret *Seder* on the first night of Pesach, like the Marrano Jews used to do in Spain," one of the girls said. "I once read a story about it. . ."

"I have an idea," another girl said, excitedly. "We will put a white sheet on the table, and I will give you the candles I have left to light in honor of the holidays."

"In my *siddur* I have the entire *Haggadah of* Pesach," the owner of the *siddur* said brightly. "We'll read together all the stories of the Exodus from Egypt."

"But the table will be completely empty without any Pesach food," one girl sighed. "If we could only have one *matzah* to remind us of the holiday. . ."

"No matter, we will celebrate the *Seder*," said the owner of the *siddur*, and she added, in a whisper, as if praying, "Perhaps a miracle will happen and we will have a *matzah* for Pesach after all."

And the miracle did happen.

Not far from the labor camp there was another large camp. It housed French prisoners of war. When the girls went out to work in the fields of the surrounding villages they could see the prisoners, dressed in army uniforms. The Nazis' treatment of the Frenchmen was infinitely better than their treatment of the Jewish girls. The prisoners were neither beaten nor wantonly tortured. But the girls knew that the prisoners were forbidden to come into contact with any Jews.

One day, the girls met a group of prisoners marching back to camp singing, and one girl noticed how one of the prisoners dropped a folded piece of paper. She furtively picked it up and brought it with her to the camp. The paper read as follows:

"My dear Jewish girls: I am a Jew just like you. This is a secret which the enemy must not discover under any circumstances. I am among the prisoners. I'll help you in any way I can. Let me know what you need. Please leave a note under the square stone outside the gate. Do not despair, girls. Do not lose hope!"

The man did not disclose his name, but the girls knew that they had come across a sympathetic Jewish heart and they decided to accept his kind offer.

In their reply, the girls asked the anonymous prisoner for some white flour for the baking of *matzos*. Early in the morning, when they went out to work, they placed the note under the stone. The next day, when they returned from work, they noticed a package which was tossed over the barbed-wire fence. In the package they found a small bag of flour, with a note attached to it:

"Congratulations, my dear girls! I envy you, for you know how to observe our holidays. I am proud of you. I got the flour from a fellow

prisoner, a Jew like myself who gets packages from home. I share
your joy of the holiday with all my heart. I hope to get you some
candy for the holiday. Be strong and of good courage!"

In the middle of the night, a few girls got up and went to work.
They posted guards at the entrance of thier barracks and at the
windows. They used bottles as rollers to flatten the dough, and
before long, having surmounted all obstacles, each girl had wrapped
a few hot, tasty *matzos* in her kerchief. The girl who owned the
siddur said:

"This is not ordinary *matzah*. This is '*Matzah Shemurah,*' guarded
matzah, for we have guarded it from all foes and destroyers!"

(from *Sparks of Glory* by Moshe Prager)

From Bondage to Freedom

◦§ Like many Soviet *ba'alei teshuvah,* Ilya (Eliyahu) Essas clearly recalls
his first religious experience at the *Seder* table:

In spring of 1972, four months after he'd begun Hebrew lessons,
his teacher, Alyosha Levin, brought a pre-Revolutionary book that
he'd never seen: a *Haggadah.* His "*rebbe*" (teacher) had himself
made only one *Seder* in his life, the year before. Now he would teach
others how to do it.

The intent young people studied for three or four lessons. They
read the *Haggadah* and studied the traditions. *Maror* was no
problem: There was plenty of bitterness in Russia. They ate it
undiluted; several actually lost their breath from its strength. For
charoses, there would be the brick-like substance that Telshe
Yeshivah had somehow smuggled in: in America, an interesting
fund-raising ploy; in the Soviet Union, a tiny link to an eternal
tradition.

Before the actual night, they held a rehearsal. How thrilled
everyone was to do everything with his own hands!

Then came the big night. Ilya Essas invited three or four friends. He
read the *Haggadah* in Hebrew and then tried to explain it. For three
hours they sat in his tiny Moscow apartment, speaking in an
unfamiliar tongue, doing unfamiliar rites.

The next day, the second day of *Yom Tov* for the Jews living outside
of Israel, seven Hebrew teachers and about twenty of their "star"
pupils gathered together for a "high-quality" *Seder.*

Like the *Seder* itself, the night was a mixture of slavery and
freedom. The participants were, at the same time, extraordinarily

proud and yet terribly afraid of the police. Some were already active refuseniks, particularly vulnerable to KGB harassment. They could all be charged with an illegal gathering, with anti-Soviet and Zionist propaganda: three to seven years.

During the *Seder* they prepared for the knock at the door. In that dangerous event, every *Haggadah* would be removed; this would be merely a social gathering of friends.

The evening passed, a mixture of tension and delight. And then came the moment of supreme danger, supreme faith. One man stood up and proudly opened the door. Rabbi Essas still remembers that moment: "When we opened the door for Elijah the Prophet, we all felt the protection of Hashem. Though none of us was observant, none of us was religious, we all felt it. We opened the door, unafraid, and looked at one another."

❀   ❀   ❀

The next year Eliyahu, already a Hebrew teacher himself, a "veteran" of Judaism after sixteen months of study, invited his pupils to his home for a *Seder*. This was the first of many *Sedarim* (pl. of *Seder*) that he was to make for others. In the future, in the 1970's and 1980's, Rabbi Essas would urge all his young, unmarried *talmidim* to lead *Sedarim* for Jews who had no knowledge, who had nothing but a strong desire to celebrate the holiday. He himself would not commit himself until the very day before *Yom Tov*, knowing that among the incessant phone calls with *halachic* queries about the holiday would come a plea for his presence. Rabbi Essas would spend the first *Seder* at home, while traveling like his forefathers in Egypt, into a spiritual desert for the second.

It wasn't easy. In April of 1983, for example, Moscow was a cold, cold place. He walked through the frigid air, the wind whipping his unprotected ears. He walked up twelve harsh, dimly lit flights of stone steps, into a small apartment, to face a crowd of almost forty people, all of them staring at him. Their faces showed a kaleidoscope of different emotions. Some were nervous, some were expectant; a few, usually dragged there by friends or spouses, were openly hostile. No one smiled. The tension was as palpable as the heat in the overcrowded room, a heat so thick that despite the frigid wind outside, brought a coating of steam to the windows.

Rabbi Essas was expected to lead this group for close to five hours, inspire them and make them forget the possibility of a KGB knock. He was to transport them from Moscow to Egypt. The place was so crowded that when it was time to lean to the left, the entire group had to do it all together around a table in a strange show of unity under tension.

Finally, in the darkness, he returned to his wife and children, who had made their *Seder* by themselves: another walk through the quiet, freezing streets. And then on *Chol HaMoed*, he reaped his reward. The telephone rang constantly with questions about the Festival, about the *Seder*, and about the Torah. And, particularly, questions on what those who attended could do next to learn more.

From that 1983 *Seder* on the twelfth floor, thirty-three participants ultimately made the commitment to a Torah life. And they, too, began to teach, and began to lead *Sedarim* for strangers.

Such was the path traveled by many Soviet Jews, a path from bondage to freedom (from *Silent Revolution* by Miriam Stark Zakon).

ఆర్క్ Selected Laws and Customs

Shabbos HaGadol
Disposing of Chametz
Laws of Bedikas Chametz
Laws of Bitul, Biur and Mechiras Chametz
The Fast of the Firstborn
Erev Pesach
Seder Preparations
When Erev Pesach Occurs on Shabbos:
    Seudos Shabbos — The Shabbos Meals
    Seudos Shabbos Options
    Seudah Shlishis
    Motzaei Shabbos
    Step by Step Guide
    Time Chart

I: Shabbos HaGadol

A. The Drashah (discourse)

The Talmud teaches us that one should ask about and hold discourse regarding the laws of Pesach from thirty days before Pesach.[1] Customarily, the Rav or another prominent Torah scholar delivers a discourse on Shabbos HaGadol — the Shabbos immediately prior to Pesach. It was in order to allow the Jewish communities in the small towns and villages (where generally no Rav was in residence) to avail themselves of this instruction that the custom evolved to schedule the discourse on Shabbos HaGadol.[2] The main purpose of this discourse is to instruct the people in the relevant laws of the upcoming holiday, such as the laws of *kashering*, the removal and disposal of chametz, the baking of matzos, and the laws of the seder. If the discourse consists merely of Talmudic discussion (*pilpul*) or homiletics (*d'rush*), the Rav has not properly fulfilled his obligation.[3]*

---

* When Erev Pesach Occurs on Shabbos:

Many authorities maintain that since all the above-mentioned procedures (except the laws of the seder) must be dealt with prior to Shabbos Erev Pesach, conducting the Shabbos HaGadol discourse on this Shabbos would not provide the people with instruction in a timely fashion. Hence, when Erev Pesach occurs on Shabbos the Shabbos HaGadol discourse is conducted on the previous Shabbos.[4]

Others, however, are of the opinion that since nowadays anyone with any inquiry regarding the laws of Pesach may seek guidance from a Rav or research the issue in halachic texts, the Shabbos HaGadol discourse no longer needs to serve its original instructional function. Rather, it is used to present Talmudic discussion (*pilpul*) or homiletic interpretations (*d'rush*). Hence, even when Erev Pesach

---

1. *Pesachim* 6a. See *Beur HaGra Orach Chaim* 429 §1 and *Beur Halachah* ad loc.

2. The rural dwellers would come to the large cities for this Shabbos and would remain there until the end of Pesach. See *Bach* O.C. 429.

3. *Mishnah Berurah* 429 §2.

4. Ibid.; *Levush* 429:1, *Ba'er Heiteiv* quoting *Maharil; Pri Megadim* ad loc., *Mishbetzos Zahav* §1, and *Shulchan Aruch HaGraz* 429:2.

B. The Haftarah of Shabbos HaGadol

According to most opinions, the *haftarah* generally read on Shabbos HaGadol is *V'Arvah LaHashem* (*Malachi* 3:4-25).[6] Two reasons are suggested by the authorities for this choice:[7]

1. In the seven-year *Shemittah* cycle, Erev Pesach of the fourth and seventh years is designated as the *she'as habiur* (time of disposal) — i.e., the deadline by which all tithes must be delivered to their proper recipients. This applies to *maaser rishon*, which is given to the Levites; *terumah* and *terumas maaser* (the *terumah* removed by the Levites from the *maaser rishon* they receive), which are given to the Kohanim; and *maasar ani* (tithe for the poor). Furthermore, all *maaser sheini* (tithe which must be eaten within the confines of Jerusalem) and *bikkurim* (first fruits) that were not brought to Jerusalem by this deadline must be destroyed.[8]

    The words of the prophet *Malachi, Bring all the tithes to the [Temple] storehouse* (ibid. v. 10), which appear in this *haftarah*, were a call for the proper disbursement or disposal of *maaser*, and thus deal with the events of the time of Erev Pesach. Hence, the choice of this portion as the *haftarah* for Shabbos HaGadol.

2. This *haftarah* portion ends with the words, *Behold I will send you Elijah the prophet before the great and fearful day of Hashem*, which refer to the great day of the final Redemption. Since this description parallels that of Moses

---

* When Erev Pesach Occurs on Shabbos:

occurs on Shabbos, the Shabbos HaGadol discourse is held on that day.[5] Every community should follow its established custom regarding the scheduling of the Shabbos HaGadol discourse.

---

5. *Aruch HaShulchan* 430:5. See also *Shulchan Aruch HaGraz* 430:3.

6. *Levush* 430; *Shulchan Aruch HaGraz* ibid.; *Mateh Moshe* 542.

7. Ibid.

8. See Mishnah, *Maaser Sheini* 5:6.

and his role in the Egyptian exodus, we read this portion as the *haftarah* of Shabbos HaGadol.[9]*

---

* When Erev Pesach Occurs on Shabbos:

There are several opinions among the authorities regarding the proper *haftarah* for Shabbos HaGadol that occurs on Erev Pesach:

a) The regular *haftarah* of the week's *parashah* is recited.[10]

This opinion maintains that the verse regarding tithes is an *exhortation* to properly dispose of them, and since one may not dispense or destroy tithes on the Sabbath itself, a warning issued on Erev Pesach which occurs on Shabbos is of no practical value. Hence, only when Shabbos HaGadol occurs before Erev Pesach do we read *V'Arvah*.[11]

b) *V'Arvah* is recited *only* when Shabbos HaGadol is Erev Pesach. This view understands that *V'Arvah's* theme of tithes was chosen as a *commemoration* (rather than an *exhortation*) of the disposal of tithes. Therefore, it was instituted as the *haftarah* only for Erev Pesach that occurs on Shabbos, which is the date on which the disposal of tithes took place in other years.[12]

c) Many are of the opinion that since the second reason (the redemption theme) for reading *V'Arvah* is appropriate regardless of whether Shabbos HaGadol occurs on Erev Pesach or not, *V'Arvah* is *always* the appropriate *haftarah* for Shabbos HaGadol.[13] This is the accepted custom.[14]

---

9. *Levush* ibid.

10. The *Gra* in *Maaseh Rav, Pesach* 176. *Aruch HaShulchan* (ibid.) states that this was the prevalent custom in his environs.

11. *Pe'ulas Sachir* to *Maaseh Rav* ad loc. [Following this line of reasoning, *V'Arvah* should apparently be recited as the *haftarah* on the *preceding* Shabbos, yet remarkably all agree that is not done.] *Maaseh Rav HaShalem*, quoting *Siach Eliyahu*, offers an alternative rationale for the *Gra's* opinion. Since the *haftarah* speaks of the coming of Elijah the prophet, an event that cannot occur on Erev Pesach (see *Eruvin* 43b), it would be an inappropriate reading on Erev Pesach which occurs on Shabbos. For further elaboration regarding the *Gra's* opinion, see *Aliba D'Hilchasa*, p. 6 fn. 31.

12. *Aruch HaShulchan* ibid. *Seder Erev Pesach Shechal Lihyos B'Shabbos* of *Maran R' Yosef Chaim Sonnenfeld*.

13. See *Siddur Beis Yaakov (R' Yaakov Emden)*, Customs of Shabbos HaGadol; *Ohr Yisrael* 430; *Yad Eliyahu* ad loc.

14. *Igros Moshe* O.C. 1:36; *Luach Ezras Torah* of *R' Yosef Eliyahu Henkin*. *Sefer Orchos Rabbeinu Baal Kehillas Yaakov* records that this was the custom of the *Steipler Gaon* and the *Chazon Ish*.

C. Other Customs Pertaining to Shabbos HaGadol

1. Most communities recite *piyutim* during *Shacharis* on Shabbos HaGadol. They are recited even when Erev Pesach occurs on Shabbos.[15]

2. It is customary to recite the Haggadah, from *Avadim Hayinu* until *Rabban Gamliel*, on Shabbos Hagadol.[16] Those who follow this custom do so even when it coincides with Erev Pesach.[17] It was the custom of the *Vilna Gaon (Gra)* not to recite the Haggadah on Shabbos HaGadol.[18]

3. *Borchi Nafshi*, customarily recited by many on Shabbosos between Succos and Pesach,[19] is not recited on Shabbos HaGadol.

II: Disposing of Chametz — Bedikah, Biur, Bitul and Mechirah

A Jew who has chametz in his possession on Pesach transgresses the Biblical prohibitions of *bal yera'eh* and *bal yimatzei* (see *Shemos* 13:7 and 12:19). The Torah commands: תַּשְׁבִּיתוּ שְׂאֹר מִבָּתֵּיכֶם, *You shall make leaven cease from your homes* (*Shemos* 12:15).

---

15. *Pri Megadim* ibid.

16. See *Rama O.C.* 430:1.

17. *Pri Megadim*, M. Z. ad loc. §1, M.B. ad loc. §2. R' *Yaakov Emden* in his Haggadah commentary, however, rules that when Shabbos HaGadol coincides with Erev Pesach, the usual Shabbos HaGadol recitation of the Haggadah should be omitted so that the mandatory recitation that night should not lose the fresh appeal of something novel, just as the Gemara forbids eating matzah on Erev Pesach for this reason. (See VI:B.) *Ohr Yisrael* 430 counters that since the Shabbos HaGadol recitation of the Haggadah stops short of the essential passages concerning *Pesach*, *Matzah* and *Maror*, without which the seder-night Haggadah requirement remains unfulfilled, the Shabbos HaGadol recitation cannot be construed as a premature performance of the mitzvah of Haggadah. It is rather analogous to eating *matzah ashirah* (e.g. egg matzah) on Erev Pesach, which is permitted since such matzah is not fit for use in fulfilling the matzah requirement of the seder night.

18. *Beur HaGra O.C.* 430, *Maaseh Rav, Pesach* 177. See *Beur Halachah* 430 s.v. *B'Minchah HaHaggadah* for explanation of the *Gra's* opinion.

19. See *Rama O.C.* 192:2. See *Tosafos* to *Menachos* 30a, s.v. *mikaan* for explanation of the custom to recite *Borchi Nafshi* (in wintertime) and *Pirkei Avos* (during summertime) after *Minchah* on Shabbos.

Ridding oneself of the chametz in his possession can be accomplished either by (a) *bedikas* and *biur chametz* (searching for and physically destroying the chametz,) or by (b) *bitul chametz* (a mental or verbal nullification or renunciation of the chametz).[1]

A. Bedikas and Biur Chametz

One searches all the places in his possession into which chametz might have been brought and then destroys the chametz. The chametz is destroyed either by burning it (the preferred way, see below), reducing it to crumbs, or grinding it and casting it to the wind.[2] One may also cast the chametz into a river or sea, but should first reduce it to crumbs or small pieces.[3] However, in deference to the opinion of the Tanna R' Yehudah, who holds that chametz must be destroyed through burning,[4] it is customary to burn the chametz.[5]

B. Bitul Chametz

Generally, *bitul chametz* is understood as the owner's renunciation of ownership of his chametz (*hefker*). Once he does so, the chametz is no longer "in his possession," even though it remains within the physical confines of his home.[6]

Bitul chametz, however, can be accomplished only before noon of Erev Pesach.[7] This is because the Torah forbids one to derive any benefit from chametz[8] from that time through the end of Pesach. Thus, the chametz in one's possession during that time is therefore classified as *issurei hana'ah* (items forbidden for all benefit), which is by definition ownerless since it has absolutely no value.[9] Since one cannot renounce what he does not own, a *bitul chametz* done after

---

1. *M.B.* 431:2. [One could also sell or give the chametz to a non-Jew, but this must be a true transfer of ownership and not a mere formality. See below, C.]

2. *O.C.* 445:1.

3. *O.C.* 445:1 with *M.B.* §5.

4. *Pesachim* 21a.

5. *Rama O.C.* 445:1.

6. See *Ran* to *Rif, Pesachim* 2a, for a lengthy discussion of the legal mechanism of *bitul chametz*.

7. "Noon" in this context refers to the halachic *chatzos*, which mots authorities define as the midpoint between sunrise and sunset.

8. *Pesachim* 21b.

9. *Pesachim* 6b and *Bava Kamma* 29b.

noon of Erev Pesach has no effect whatever. [The *de facto* suspension of ownership effected by this prohibition, which takes effect at noon on Erev Pesach, does *not* serve to release a person from the prohibition of having chametz in his possession. For, as the Gemara teaches, chametz on Pesach is one of the items that a person does not own from a monetary standpoint, but which the Torah considers in his possession *for purposes of liability* (in this case, liability for violating the prohibition against having chametz in one's possession on Pesach).[10] Thus, a person can use *bitul chametz* to avoid having chametz in his possession on Pesach only if he performs the *bitul* while the chametz is still his from a *monetary* standpoint (in which case his renunciation is still meaningful) — that is, before noon of Erev Pesach.] [Noon is the deadline for *bitul chametz* only according to Biblical law. Rabbinically, however, chametz becomes forbidden for all benefit one hour before noon,[11] and *bitul chametz* must therefore be performed before the onset of this Rabbinic prohibition.[12]

In practice, *bitul chametz* is performed much earlier than the deadline — see IV:A1.]

While either *bedikas/biur chametz* or *bitul chametz* is a valid way of avoiding the Biblical prohibition against having chametz in one's possession on Pesach, it is Rabbinically incumbent upon a person to do both. The Rabbis did not want a person to rely solely on *bitul chametz*, since mental or verbal nullification may sometimes be insincere (e.g. where the person has valuable chametz in his possession, which he does not wholeheartedly renounce or consider null "like the dust of the earth" [part of the *bitul chametz*

---

10. *Pesachim* ibid., *Rashi* ad loc.

11. The "hour" meant here is the variable hour [שָׁעָה זְמַנִּית], whose length varies with the time of year. A variable hour is 1/12 of the daylight hours (and is thus shorter than sixty minutes in the winter and longer in the summer). There is disagreement among the authorities regarding how the day is reckoned with regard to these laws. Some rule that the day is reckoned as beginning with dawn and ending with the emergence of the stars (see *Magen Avraham*, O.C. 443 §3). Others rule that it is reckoned as starting at sunrise and ending at sundown (see *Beur HaGra* to O.C. 459 s.v. *U'Shiur mil* and O.C. 443:4). Ideally one should comply with the first, more stringent, view (see O.C. 443, M.B. §8; see, however, *Igros Moshe* O.C. 1:24).

12. O.C. 432:2.

formula]), rendering the *bitul* ineffective and leaving the person in violation of having chametz in his possession on Pesach. Moreover, even when the *bitul* is sincere, the person might forget and eat on Pesach the chametz that he has nullified, since he is not used to considering chametz (which is permitted the rest of the year) a forbidden substance. Therefore, the Rabbis insisted that one search for and destroy the chametz in his possession. Since, however, the search might overlook some chametz that is in a person's possession, the Rabbis required that one perform *bitul chametz* in addition to his search.[13]

C. Mechiras Chametz

Technically, one could remove the chametz in his possession by selling or giving it to a non-Jew. This is effective even if the Jew knows that the non-Jew intends to return the chametz intact after Pesach.[14] However, the gift or sale must be a real one and not just a mere formality,[15] and it should not be done on a conditional basis.[16] Though a real sale or gift of the chametz to a non-Jew is a perfectly legitimate means of removing chametz from one's possession,[17] some prefer to avoid this method[18] for fear that one or both of the parties will not really take the transaction seriously, knowing full well that the chametz will be restored to the Jew after Pesach.[19]

---

13. *M.B.* 431:2, based on *Pesachim* 5b and *Tosafos* to 2a.

14. *Chasam Sofer* (Responsa, O.C. 113) writes that the use of *mechiras chametz* is of unquestionable halachic validity, even if both parties are aware that the Jew would really want the chametz returned after Pesach.

15. *O.C.* 448:2.

16. Ibid. If the gift or sale is conditional, one runs the risk of the condition not being fulfilled, thereby voiding the transaction retroactively, in which case it will emerge that the Jew did indeed have chametz in his possession on Pesach and violated the relevant prohibitions.

17. See *Maharam Schick*, Responsa O.C. 45; *Arugas HaBosem*, Responsa O.C. 103.

18. See *Maaseh Rav* Pesach 180.

19. See *Seder Mechiras Chametz K'Hilchasa* 1:10 for an extensive listing of opinions.

III: Laws of Bedikas Chametz — Searching for Chametz

1. Generally, on the night of the 14th of Nissan (the night before Pesach), one searches all the places in his domain into which chametz may have been brought.[1*]

2. The search obligation applies to all householders, including women living alone. If one owns a place of business, he must conduct a search there as well.[4] Those who spend Pesach at a hotel and arrive there before the time of bedikah should consult a competent halachic authority.

3. Before commencing the search one recites the *berachah*: בָּרוּךְ אַתָּה ה' אֱלֹקֵינוּ מֶלֶךְ הָעוֹלָם אֲשֶׁר קִדְּשָׁנוּ בְּמִצְוֹתָיו וְצִוָּנוּ עַל בִּעוּר חָמֵץ, *Blessed are You, HASHEM, our G-d, King of the Universe, Who has sanctified us by his commandments, and commanded us concerning the removal of chametz.*[5] The *berachah* mentions the removal of (rather than search for) chametz even though the removal (i.e. destruction) will not take place until the following morning, because the ultimate purpose of the search is the subsequent removal of chametz.[6] Just as with other mitzvos, one may not interpose between the *berachah* and the beginning of the search with extraneous talk; if one did talk, he must recite the *berachah* again. Moreover, one

---

* When Erev Pesach Occurs on Shabbos:

The search for chametz is pushed back to Thursday night, the 13th of Nissan.[2] This pushed-back search is subject to the same rules as searches conducted on the 14th of Nissan in most years.[3]

---

1. *O.C.* 433:3. *M.B.* §19 writes that in a house where young children are present one must be most vigilant in searching all places.

2. *O.C.* 444:1.

3. These laws are found in *Shulchan Aruch, O.C* Chs. 431-434.

4. One should consult a halachic authority as to when and how the place of business should be searched.

5. *O.C.* 432:1.

6. *M.B.* ibid. §2. See *Gilyonei HaShas, Pesachim* 7b, who explains the term *biur* in the sense of removal as in *Devarim* 26:13. Hence *bedikah* is in fact *biur*.

should refrain from extraneous talk during the entire search.[7] It is customary to put out [ten] pieces of *chametz* in advance, which are to be found in the course of the search, so that the *berachah* should not have been recited in vain in the event no other chametz is found.[8] The search must be done with a candle.[9] However, due to the risks involved in searching with a candle, many authorities suggest reciting the *berachah* and beginning the search with a candle and then switching to a flashlight or the like.[10]

4. One should begin the search immediately upon nightfall, as defined by צֵאת הַכּוֹכָבִים, *the emergence of the stars.* [There are various views concerning the precise time of "the emergence of the stars," and each person should follow the tradition of his community in this matter.]

5. Out of fear that one will become preoccupied and neglect his obligation to search for chametz, it is forbidden to begin any type of work within the half hour prior to this time.[11] Similarly one may not take a haircut, enter the bathhouse, or do other such tasks which have the potential to become prolonged.[12]

6. While it is permitted to commence work earlier than a half hour in advance of the time for the search, one must cease all work when the actual time for the search arrives.[13]

7. Some authorities forbid one to commence private Torah study within the aforementioned half hour,[14] while others

---

7. *O.C.* 432:1; *M.B.* ad loc.

8. *Rama O.C.* 432:2. However, if one does not do so, the *berachah* is still valid. See *M.B.* ad loc. §13.

9. *O.C.* 433:2. See *Shearim HaMetzuyanim B'Halachah* 111.

10. *R' Moshe Feinstein* quoted by *R' Shimon Eider* in *Hilchos Pesach* Vol. I p. 86, fns. 81 and 82.

11. *O.C.* 431:2, *M.B.* §5, *Shulchan Aruch HaGraz O.C.* 431:5.

12. *M.B.* ibid.; see *O.C.* 232:2.

13. *Rama O.C.* 431:2. *Shulchan Aruch HaGraz* 431:6 explains that despite the fact that he commenced working prior to the time of obligation, while work was still permitted, nonetheless, by not ceasing at *tzeis hakochavim* he ignores the enactment of the Sages who deemed *tzeis hakochavim* as the optimal time for the search.

14. *M.B.* ibid. §7 ibid. in the name of *Magen Avraham* and *Shulchan Aruch HaGraz.*

permit it. However, one must cease his study as of *tzeis hakochavim* in order to perform the search.[15] According to all opinions, one may attend a regularly scheduled public class until *tzeis hakochavim*.[16]

Likewise, according to all opinions, if one appointed another person to remind him at *tzeis hakochavim* of the obligation to search, he may begin a private Torah study session even within the half hour.[17]

8. In all of the aforementioned instances in which Torah study is permitted, it is permitted only when the study is not conducted in an in-depth manner. In-depth study (*pilpul*), by nature, causes an involvement and preoccupation that has the potential to distract one from the incumbent search obligation, and is hence forbidden.[18]

9. Eating is forbidden within the half hour prior to *tzeis hakochavim*. A light refreshment, such as a small amount of bread or cake (less than the volume of an egg) or an unlimited amount of fruit, or the like, is permitted during this half hour.[19] However, as of *tzeis hakochavim*, only a small amount of fruit is permitted.[20]

10. One who generally *davens Maariv* with a *minyan* at *tzeis hakochavim* should do so before the search for chametz,

---

15. *Chok Yaakov* and *Magen HaAlef* 431:2.

16. *M.B.* ibid., *Shoneh Halachos* 431:6. See *Shulchan Aruch HaGraz* 431:9, who permits a public study session in *halachah* (as opposed to in-depth study) to continue even past *tzeis hakochavim*.

17. *M.B.* ibid.

18. Ibid.

19. *O.C.* 431:1; *M.B.* §6.

20. See *Beur Halachah* 431 s.v. *v'lo yochal*. Once the time of the search arrives (*tzeis hakochavim*), it is improper to delay the search even by mere inactivity and certainly not with work or eating. In this sense the search for chametz is more stringent than the recitation of *Krias Shema*. For while it is preferable to recite the *Shema* immediately at *tzeis hakochavim*, there is no *obligation* to do so; therefore, only a full meal is forbidden at that time, but light refreshment is permitted (see *O.C.* 235, *M.B.* §16). In the case of *bedikas chametz*, however, where the primary obligation is to begin immediately at *tzeis hakochavim*, even the delay involved in the consumption of larger amounts of fruit is prohibited.

since assembling a *minyan* later may be difficult.[21]

11. If one who generally prays with a later *minyan* plans to pray privately this night, he should delegate someone else to search for chametz at *tzeis hakochavim* while he prays.[22] If no such delegate is available, he should pray first and then conduct the search.[23]

12. Regarding one who generally *davens Maariv* privately, there is disagreement among the authorities whether prayer or the search for chametz take precedence.[24] Some are of the opinion that since this individual generally prays privately, we need not be concerned that due to the search he will forget to pray. Hence these authorities give precedence to the search.[25] Others[26] give precedence to the *Maariv* prayers based on the Talmudic dictum: "Frequent and infrequent — the frequent takes precedence."[27] One may follow either opinion.[28]

13. If one forgot to search on the night designated for the search, he must do so on the next day.[29] He is forbidden to do any of the previously mentioned items (see 5) prior to conducting this search.[30] This daytime search must be

---

21. *M.B.* 431 §8. And we are not afraid of the *Maariv* prayers being prolonged, causing one to neglect the search.

22. Ibid. In this fashion he will fulfill both obligations (i.e. *Maariv* and the search) at the proper time.

23. Ibid. [Since he generally does not pray privately, we are concerned that he may forget to pray if he conducts the search first.]

24. *M.B.* ibid.

25. *Chayei Adam* 119:7; *Maharsham; Aruch HaShulchan* 431:31. *Shulchan Aruch HaGraz* 431:6 explains that by delaying the recitation of *Shema* and *Maariv* until later, one transgresses no Rabbinic enactment; although it is *praiseworthy* to recite *Shema* at *tzeis hakochavim*, it may be done until midnight. However, one who delays the search for chametz beyond *tzeis hakochavim* transgresses the Rabbinic enactment that designates *tzeis hakochavim* as the *primary* time for this mitzvah.

26. *Chok Yaakov, Eliyahu Rabbah, Mekor Chaim* ad loc.

27. *Berachos* 51b.

28. *Shaar HaTziun* ad loc. §11.

29. *O.C.* 435:1.

30. *M.B.* 431 §5.

conducted with a candle[31] and the appropriate blessing (*al biur chametz*) is recited.[32]*

---

* When Erev Pesach Occurs on Shabbos:

When Erev Pesach occurs on Shabbos and one neglected his obligation to search until Friday night, he should conduct the search[33] in the following manner:

All areas that can be properly searched with the electric light already illuminating the room, as well as items such as books, gloves, pockets, and movable objects from which all chametz can be shaken out,[34] should be searched on Friday night.[35] All areas that contain nooks and crevices must be searched by candlelight and there is thus no way to search them on Friday night.

Areas that are exposed to great amounts of sunlight [such as a portico with only three walls (*achsadra*), areas opposite windows[36] or any similar such places] should be searched on Shabbos morning.

All the chametz discovered during the Friday night and Shabbos morning searches should be given to a non-Jew, to an animal (e.g. dog) who will consume it, or else the chametz may be flushed down the toilet.[37]

All searches conducted on Shabbos day should be conducted with

---

31. *Ba'er Heiteiv* 435 §1. See *M.B.* ad loc. §4.

32. *Shulchan Aruch HaGraz* 435:1.

33. Even though one cannot use a candle for this search, he must fulfill the obligation to search for chametz. See *Halachos Ketanos* 194, cited in *Shaarei Teshuvah* 433 §1.

34. *Maharsham* glosses 433:2, *Shaarei Teshuvah* 433. See Responsa *Shevet HaLevi* 1:136.

35. Care should be taken to avoid moving *muktzeh* objects. See *Aliba D'Hilchasa* p. 28 fn. 125 for further clarification of this matter.

36. *M.B.* 434 §43 writes: "If one did not search a *beis haknesses* or *beis hamidrash* on the night of the fourteenth of Nissan, he may do so during the next day. He does not need a candle. Since they have many windows and much light they are considered like an *achsadra* (portico)." Accordingly, it would seem that our rooms, lit with electric lights, may likewise be checked by electric light since the illumination is at least equal to that provided by daylight shed through the windows of the *beis haknesses*. [Of course, during the week, a candle is needed.]

While *M.B.* ibid. writes that glass panes in the windows disqualify the *beis haknesses* from being considered like an *achsadra*, see *Daas Torah* 434 §1 (citing *Daas Kedoshim*) who writes that our windows, which are fully transparent, do not prevent the area within from being treated like an *achsadra*.

37. See *M.B.* 444 §21.

14. If one did not conduct the search before the onset of Yom Tov, the proper course of action is as follows:

(a) If one performed *bitul chametz* prior to the sixth hour** one should not search on Yom Tov proper, but rather conduct the search on *Chol HaMoed*[39] and burn whatever chametz he finds at that time.

(b) Regarding one who did not perform *bitul chametz*, there is a divergence of opinion among the authorities. Some are of the opinion that one should conduct the search as soon as possible (even on Yom Tov)[40] and dispose of the chametz by flushing it down the toilet.[41] Many authorities even allow one to burn any chametz discovered during this search.[42]

Other opinions hold that the search should be delayed until *Chol HaMoed*.[43] A competent halachic authority should be consulted.

---

the appropriate *berachah, al biur chametz.* Regarding the search conducted on Friday night, some doubt exists regarding reciting the *berachah.* Therefore one should not recite the *berachah.*[38]

** See II:B fn. 11 for clarification of the halachic usage of the term "hour."

---

38. See *Aliba D'Hilchasa* ibid.

39. M.B. 435 §3, *Shaar HaTziun* ad loc. §9.

40. M.B. ibid.

41. M.B. 446 §6.

42. M.B. ibid.

43. M.B. 435 §3.

IV: Laws of Bitul, Biur and Mechiras Chametz

A. Bitul Chametz — Renouncing Ownership of Chametz

1. The *bitul chametz* formula is recited at night after the completion of the search.[1] It is done at this time to provide for the contingency that one might forget to do so on the morrow before the sixth hour.[2]

2. Since, of course, one does not want to include in his nullification the chametz he intends to eat or burn the next day, the declaration recited at night speaks only of that chametz which is in one's possession of which he is unaware.[3]

3. The *bitul* formula may be recited in any language.[4] If one recites it in Hebrew he must at least understand the general intent of the formula (the renunciation of ownership of the chametz). If he does not understand it at all and is under the impression that he is reciting some type of prayer, he has not fulfilled the obligation of *bitul chametz*.[5]

4. Generally, a second declaration of *bitul chametz* is recited in the morning after the burning of the chametz but prior to the onset of the sixth hour.[6] This daytime *bitul* includes both discovered *and* undiscovered chametz.[7]*

---

* When Erev Pesach Occurs on Shabbos:

As noted previously the search is conducted on Thursday night and the burning on Friday.[8] However, the daytime *bitul* is omitted after

---

1. O.C. 434:2.
2. *Pesachim* 6b, *Rashi* ad loc. s.v. *pasha*. See O.C. 434:2, M.B. §11 and *Shaar HaTziun* ad loc.
3. O.C. 434:2, M.B. ad loc. §7. See *Ba'er Heiteiv* ad loc. for the complete text of the nighttime *bitul* declaration.
4. *Rama* ad loc.
5. M.B. ad loc. §9.
6. O.C. ibid., *Rama* ad loc.
7. O.C. 434:3.
8. O.C. 444:1, M.B. §11.

B. Biur Chametz — Disposal of Chametz

1. The optimal way to dispose of chametz is to burn it.[12] Generally, the burning of chametz is done before the onset of the sixth hour in order to assure (a) that one recites the *bitul chametz* formula (which follows immediately) while the chametz is still his and thus he is still able to do *bitul* on it, and (b) that he will perform the mitzvah of *biur chametz* on his own chametz.[13]*

When Erev Pesach Occurs on Shabbos:

burning the chametz on Friday, since one wants to retain in his possession all the chametz food needed for his Shabbos meals.[9] [One who will dispose of all chametz on Friday and use only non-chametz foods for his Shabbos meals should recite the usual *bitul* formula on Friday.[10]]

Instead, when Erev Pesach occurs on Shabbos, the second *bitul chametz* declaration (which includes both discovered and undiscovered chametz) is made on Shabbos morning after the meals have been eaten and all remaining chametz has been disposed of.[11] Like every year, this *bitul chametz* must be made before the end of the fifth hour.

❧ ❧ ❧

The disposal (by burning) of *chametz* he is not keeping for use on Shabbos takes place on Friday,[14] since one may not burn anything on Shabbos. One should burn the chametz on Friday before the sixth hour, so as not to lead to confusion in other years.[15]

If one forgot to burn the chametz at this time, he may burn it anytime before Shabbos.[16] Once Shabbos begins, however, he may not burn the chametz. Rather, he should dispose of it by flushing it down the toilet or by giving it to a gentile.[17]

---

9. *Rama O.C.* 444:2, M.B. §10.
10. Responsa *Yechaveh Daas* 91 §11.
11. See fn. 9.
12. *Tur O.C.* 445, *Rama O.C.* 445:1, M.B. §6.
13. *O.C.* 445:1, M.B. §7.
14. *O.C.* 444:2.
15. *O.C.* 444:2.
16. See *Aliba D'Hilchasa* p. 49.
17. *O.C.* 444:5, M.B. §21.

C. Mechiras Chametz — Selling the Chametz

The halachic issues involved in the sale of chametz are extremely intricate and complex. It is therefore of the utmost importance to engage a Rav or a *beis din* fully competent in the intricacies of these laws to execute the sale.

1. The sale of chametz must be executed any time before the sixth hour of Erev Pesach, which is when the prohibition to benefit from chametz begins. One may obviously not sell the chametz after this time, since it is no longer his to sell.*

---

* When Erev Pesach Occurs on Shabbos:

Since the chametz cannot be sold on that day, it is sold, instead, on Friday.

Now, as previously explained (see IV:A4), when Erev Pesach occurs on Shabbos, one should still burn the chametz on Friday before the sixth hour, to prevent confusion in other years. The authorities discuss whether the same reasoning is applied to the sale of chametz on Friday, when Erev Pesach occurs on Shabbos. Some authorities suggest conducting the sale of chametz at the usual time of day for the above-noted reason.[18]

Other authorities allow the sale of chametz in such years to be executed, if necessary, even later than the sixth hour, immediately prior to Shabbos.[19] One should, of course, follow the custom of the Rav or *talmid chacham* who arranges the sale.

If one who possesses a considerable amount of chametz forgot to sell it before Shabbos, a competent halachic authority must be consulted. Some authorities permit the chametz to be given on Shabbos, as an unconditional gift to a non-Jew.[20] The non-Jew must make the appropriate *kinyan* (acquisition act) and bring the chametz into his own domain. One must be careful not to stipulate in any way that the non-Jew not partake of the chametz, or that he return it after Pesach.

---

18. Responsa *Maharam Schick O.C.* 45. See *Chok Yisrael* 13 for an extensive discussion and listing of opinions.

19. *Orchos Chaim* 444:4 citing *Chasam Sofer* and others.

20. *M.B.* 444 §20.

V: The Fast of the Firstborn

1. Since the Jewish firstborns were saved from the plague visited upon the Egyptian firstborns,[1] it is customary for all Jewish firstborn males [whether firstborn of mother or father] to fast on Erev Pesach.[2] A father fasts in place of his male firstborn who is still a minor. If the father is a firstborn (and must fast himself) the mother should fast in place of her son.[3] If this is difficult for her, they may rely on the father's fasting on behalf of both himself and his son. If the woman is pregnant or nursing and experiences difficulty fasting, she need not fast even if the father is not present or not fasting. A woman within thirty days after childbirth *may not* fast.[4]

2. A firstborn who fasts recites the *Aneinu* prayer in the *Shomei'a Tefillah* blessing at the *Minchah* service. If ten firstborn males pray together and one of them leads the services, he recites *Aneinu* during the reader's repetition, as would be done on any other personal fast (*taanis yachid*). It is preferable, however, that a non-firstborn lead the *Minchah* service, since according to some authorities it is inappropriate during Nissan to make mention of a personal fast during the reader's repetition.[5] *Vayechal*, the regular Torah reading for fast days, is not read.[6]

3. One who has a headache or eye pain is not required to fast. Preferably, however, he should restrict his food intake to occasional snacks and not eat a full meal.[7] This leniency may also be followed by one who fears that, as a result of

---

1. See *Shemos* 11:4-7, 12:29-30.
2. *Yerushalmi, Pesachim* 10:1; *Maseches Sofrim* 21:3; *Tur O.C.* 470; *Beis Yosef* ad loc. *Birkei Yosef* sees the fast as a way of publicizing the miraculous saving of the Jewish firstborns.
3. *Rama O.C.* 470:2.
4. *M. B.* ad loc. §9; see *Shoneh Halachos* ad loc. §3.
5. *O.C.* 4701:1; *M.B.* 2.
6. *Aruch HaShulchan O.C.* 470:3.
7. *M.B.* 470 §2. See *Yeshuos Yaakov O.C.* 470 §1.

the fast, he will be unable to properly fulfill the mitzvos of drinking the four cups and eating matzah or *maror* at the seder.[8]

4. The preceding discussion regarding the fast of the firstborn assumes that in practice firstborns do fast, which — according to many authorities — is the preferred practice.[9] However, since this fast is a custom rather than a Rabbinic enactment, the prevalent custom is for the firstborn to participate in a *siyum* (the completion of a significant portion of Torah study — see next paragraph) or any other *seudas mitzvah* (mitzvah meal, such as one celebrating a *bris* [circumcision] or a *pidyon haben*) and thereby exempt himself from the fast.[10]

5. The *siyum* referred to is one that celebrates the completion (*siyum*) of a Talmudic tractate, an order of Mishnah,[11] or even a book of Scriptures (if the book was studied in depth with classic commentators).[12]

Even though the firstborn did not himself participate in the study of the book being completed, he may participate in the *siyum* by being in attendance and listening as the final portion of the book is taught or read by the one conducting the *siyum*.[13] The firstborn may then partake of the celebratory meal.[14] He may not eat before the *siyum*.[15] However, his

---

8. *M.B.* ibid.

9. See *Aruch HaShulchan* 470:5, who finds difficulty justifying preempting the fast by means of a *siyum*. See also *Mikra'ei Kodesh, Pesach* Ch. 22. For a lengthy discussion of the matter, see Responsa *Minchas Yitzchak* Vol. 8:48. *Maharsham* (glosses O.C. 470:1) quotes *Teshuvah MeAhavah*, Vol. 3, which cites a proclamation of *Noda B'Yehudah* and his *beis din* that firstborns must fast and may not eat at a *siyum* on Erev Pesach.

10. *M.B.* 470 §9.

11. See glosses of *Maharsham* 551:10 and *Orchos Chaim* (Spinka) 551:35.

12. *Igros Moshe* O.C. 1:157. See also Responsa *Pnei Mavin* O.C. 103 and *Maharsham* ibid.

13. R' *Yisrael Veltz* (*Dayan* of Budapest) in his *Seder Erev Pesach* (in Yiddish) writes that it is proper to offer a gratuity to the Rav or Torah scholar who conducts the *siyum*.

14. *M.B.* 470:9. It would seem that the firstborn must *hear* the *siyum* in order to be allowed to eat. *Siddur Pesach K'Hilchaso* reports such a ruling in the name of *HaGaon R' Yosef Shalom Eliyashiv, shlita*.

15. *Magen Avraham* O.C. 568 §10 cited in *M. B.* ad loc. §18.

participation in the *siyum* cancels the fast and allows him to eat for the remainder of the day.[16]

If a firstborn was not present at the *siyum*, he may not have food from the meal sent to his home to partake of it there.[17]*

---

* When Erev Pesach Occurs on Shabbos:

The fast of the firstborn may not be observed on that day since fasting on Shabbos is prohibited.[18] Three opinions are cited by the authorities regarding the rescheduling of the fast:

(a) The fast is observed on Thursday.[19]

(b) The fast is preempted altogether.[20]

(c) The fast is held on Friday.[21]

The prevalent custom is to fast on Thursday.[22] If one forgot to fast on Thursday, a competent halachic authority should be consulted.[23]

This custom presents a unique difficulty. Immediately at nightfall on Thursday, which is when the fast ends, one is obligated to search

---

16. Ibid. See *Aliba D'Hilchasa* p. 15 fn. 74..

17. See *Rama O.C.* 568:2; *Eliyahu Rabbah* 551:26.

18. See O.C. 288, which delineates exceptions to the prohibition of fasting on Shabbos.

19. *O.C.* 470:2; *M.B.* §6. *Aruch HaShulchan* 470:4 explains that when the fast must be rescheduled, it is preferable not to reschedule it to Friday so as not to cause one to enter Shabbos in pain and distress. See also *Midrash Tanchuma, Bereishis* 3 (regarding *Taanis Esther*): "When the 14th of Adar occurs on Sunday one is forbidden to fast on Friday due to the efforts necessary for Shabbos preparations. Since the main agenda of a fast day is the recitation of *selichos* and extra prayers for Heavenly mercy, it will impede properly honoring the Shabbos. The honoring of Shabbos, which is a Biblical obligation, outweighs the obligation to fast, which is of Rabbinic origin. Therefore, we reschedule the fast for Thursday." *Mikra'ei Kodesh* 23 in *Harerei Kodesh* 1 cites this *midrash* as a basis for the Thursday rescheduling of the fast of the firstborn.

20. *O.C.* ibid. *M.B.* §7. Since this fast is a custom rather than an obligation, it is preempted rather than rescheduled if it cannot be kept on the proper date.

21. *Birkei Yosef* 470. See *Maharam Provencia* and *Meiri* cited in *Kaf HaChaim* 470:20.

22. *Rama O.C.* 470:2, *Shulchan Aruch HaGraz* 470:7. *Chazon Ovadiah, Hilchos Erev Pesach* §10, writes that this is the Sephardic custom. However, in pressing circumstances, Sephardim may rely on the opinion of *Shulchan Aruch* (see fn. 7) and not fast.

23. See *Mikra'ei Kodesh* Ch. 23 in *Harerei Kodesh* 2. See *Aliba D'Hilchasa* p. 17 fn. 87.

VI: Erev Pesach

A. The Prohibition of Chametz on Erev Pesach

While according to most authorities, one does not transgress the prohibitions of *bal yera'eh* and *bal yimatzei* until the night of the 15th of Nissan,[1] one is nonetheless obligated by force of a *positive*

---

* When Erev Pesach Occurs on Shabbos:

for chametz (see III:4) and once the time for the search has arrived, one may not eat until he has fulfilled the mitzvah.[24] Thus, the firstborn must prolong the fast.

However, if a firstborn finds difficulty in prolonging the fast, he should partake of a snack (i.e. bread less than the volume of an egg or any quantity of fruit)[25] prior to commencing his search for chametz. Alternatively he may appoint someone to conduct the search in his stead and is then permitted to eat a full meal.[26]

Because of the rescheduling of the fast, the law regarding illness is even more lenient, and a firstborn suffering even minimal discomfort need not fast. Instead, he should make a donation to charity, according to his ability, as a redemption of the fast. Ideally, he should try to participate in a *siyum* and thereby be exempt from the fasting requirement (see below).[27]

Attending a *siyum* on Thursday[28] allows the firstborn to eat on both Thursday and Friday.[29] Some authorities suggest making a *siyum* on both days.[30]

---

24. See III fn. 20.

25. *O.C.* 431, *M.B.* §6.

26. *M.B.* 470 §6.

27. *Maran R' Yosef Chaim Sonnenfeld*, §1.

28. *Chok Yisrael; Mikra'ei Kodesh, Pesach*, Ch. 23. See also *Yeshuos Yaakov* 470 §3.

29. See *Aliba D'Hilchasa* p. 18 fn. 88.

30. *Orchos Rabbeinu* reports that this was the custom of the *Kehillas Yaakov (Steipler Gaon)* and is followed by his son, *HaGaon R' Chaim Kanievsky, shlita*.

1. *Rambam, Chametz U'Matzah* 3:7 and *Maggid Mishneh* ad loc.; *Levush* 431:1. See *Chok Yaakov* 443 §4. *Magen Avraham* 443 §1 and *M.B.* 443 §1 concur. See *Shaar HaTziun* ad loc. §2.

Rashi, Pesachim 4a s.v. *bein l'Rebbi Meir*, holds that the *bal yera'eh* and *bal yimatzei* prohibitions begin at the sixth hour. See also *Rashi, Bava Kamma* 29b s.v.

commandment to remove his chametz by midday (6 hours) of Erev Pesach.[2] This obligation is derived[3] from the following verse:

For a seven-day period shall you eat matzos, but on the previous (lit: first) day you shall make leaven cease from your homes; for anyone who eats leavened food — that soul shall be cut off from Israel, from the first day to the seventh day (Shemos 12:15).

The Talmud[4] clarifies the time frame of this obligation by means of a second Biblical verse: *You shall not slaughter My blood offering* [the *pesach*] *while in possession of leavened food (Shemos 34:25).* This verse teaches that at midday (when the *pesach* offering may be slaughtered) one may no longer possess chametz. By inference, the obligation to nullify or destroy the chametz is also effective at this time. Moreover, chametz is Biblically forbidden for all benefit from this time onward.

The Sages extended the scope of these prohibitions as follows: Chametz may not be eaten on Erev Pesach from the beginning of the fifth hour.[5] However, one may derive benefit from chametz until the beginning of the sixth hour.[6]

B. The Prohibition of Eating Matzah on Erev Pesach

On Erev Pesach, one may not eat matzah that is fit for use in fulfilling the mitzvah of eating matzah on Pesach.[7] The *Talmud Yerushalmi* sees this as analogous to one cohabiting with his betrothed at the home of his father-in-law[8] (i.e. without the benefit of

---

m'sheish shaos. See *Shaar HaTziun* ibid. Responsa *Noda B'Yehudah* O.C. Vol. 1:20 attempts to equate the position of *Rambam* with that of *Rashi*.

2. O.C. 443:1.

3. *Pesachim* 4b.

4. Ibid. This follows the position of Rava. See *Rambam, Chametz U'Matzah* 2:1.

5. *Rambam, Chametz U'Matzah* 1:9. O.C. 443:1.

6. Ibid.

7. *Rama* O.C. 371:2.

8. *Pesachim* 10:1, quoted in *Tosafos* to *Pesachim* 99a s.v. *v'lo yochal. Shibbolei HaLeket* 208 explains the analogy: One who cohabits with his betrothed does so without the benefit of the seven blessings (*sheva berachos*) associated with *nisuin*, which in fact permit this cohabitation ("a bride without [seven] *berachos* is forbidden to her husband like a *niddah*" — see *Kallah* 1:1). Similarly, a matzah is prohibited until one has recited the following seven *berachos*. (1) *Borei Prei HaGafen* (of *Kiddush*);

the seven blessings associated with *nisuin*, the final stage of marriage).

Rambam explains the reason for the prohibition as a means of differentiation; that is, to indicate that unlike matzah consumption prior to Pesach, which is optional, the eating of matzah on the seder night is in fulfillment of a Biblical mitzvah.[9] One who transgresses this Rabbinic prohibition is liable for *makkas mardus* (lashes for violating a Rabbinic precept).[10]

Regarding the time frame of this prohibition, there is disagreement among the authorities. Some hold that this prohibition begins from the night of the 14th of Nissan;[11] others hold that it begins at dawn (*amud hashachar*),[12] while yet others hold that it does not begin until the onset of the fifth hour of the day.[13]

Many practice the custom of refraining from eating matzah as of *Rosh Chodesh Nissan*.[14]

C. Matzah Ashirah — "Egg Matzah"

The Mishnah states: "On the eve of Pesach close to the *Minchah* [period] a person may not eat until it becomes dark."[15] This prohibition must refer to foods other than leavened bread, since chametz is already forbidden from the beginning of the fifth hour. Nor does the Mishnah refer to matzah, since matzah, too, is already forbidden prior to that time (as previously noted). Consequently, the

---

(2) *Kiddush* (*M'kadesh Yisrael V'HaZmanim*); (3) *Shehechianu*; (4) *Borei Pri HaAdamah* (recited on *karpas*); (5) *Borei Pri HaGafen* (on the second cup); (6) *HaMotzi*; and (7) *Al Achilas Matzah* (recited on the matzah). Interestingly, *Maaseh Rav* 191 uses the expression — *and then after these seven [berachos] we reveal the face of the bride* — regarding eating matzah at the seder.

9. *Chametz U'Matzah* 6:12. [This is comparable to the *shofar*-blowing during the month of Elul. On Erev Rosh Hashanah this is suspended in order to differentiate between customary and obligatory blowing. See *O.C.* 581:3; *M.B.* §24.]

10. Ibid.

11. *Magen Avraham* 471 §6. See *Chok Yaakov* ad loc. §7.

12. *Rama O.C.* 471:2; *M.B.* §12; *Rambam*, *Chametz U'Matzah* 6:12; *Maggid Mishneh* ad loc.

13. *Rosh* and *Ran* to *Pesachim* 49a, *Baal HaMaor* as interpreted by *Ran* ad loc.

14. *M.B.* ibid.

15. *Pesachim* 99b.

Mishnah must refer to other foods, which would otherwise be permitted on the afternoon of Erev Pesach.[16]

Tosafos[17] explain that the Mishnah refers to מַצָּה עֲשִׁירָה, rich matzah, i.e. matzah made with flour and eggs or fruit juices. Since such matzah is not acceptable for the mitzvah, it may be eaten on Erev Pesach. Nonetheless, such matzah should not be eaten from close to the time for Minchah and onward.

Rosh[18] states that it was the custom of Rabbeinu Tam to eat matzah ashirah for the third Shabbos meal. It emerges, then, that both Tosafos and Rosh permit eating matzah ashirah until the tenth hour of Erev Pesach.

According to Rambam,[19] however, the Mishnah refers to fruits and vegetables. One may eat only small amounts of these items, but he may not satiate himself with these foods. According to the Gra,[20] Rambam forbids eating matzah ashirah the entire day of Erev Pesach.

Rama[21] states that since the Ashkenazic custom is not to eat matzah ashirah on Pesach,[22] one may not eat matzah ashirah from the fifth hour of Erev Pesach.[23]

According to most authorities one may eat kneidlach (matzah balls) on Erev Pesach until the tenth hour.[24]

---

16. The Mishnah, however, forbids eating them at this time so that one will fulfill his obligation to eat matzah that night with appetite (see below).

17. Ad loc. s.v. lo.

18. Pesachim 10:1.

19. Chametz U'Matzah 6:12.

20. Beur HaGra 444 §7.

21. O.C. 444:1. See Kaf HaChaim 471 §15 regarding the Sephardic custom.

22. See M.B. 462 §15 for the reason behind the Ashkenazic custom.

23. Igros Moshe 1:155 rules in accordance with Rama.

Maharal (Gevuros HaShem 48) forbids matzah ashirah on Erev Pesach for a different reason. He posits that there are two elements to the mitzvah of matzah: (1) "In the evening [of Pesach] you shall eat matzah" (Shemos 12:18), and (2) matzah is referred to as lechem oni "poor bread" (Devarim 16:3). While matzah ashirah "enriched" with fruit juice or the like is not lechem oni, it is matzah and as such is forbidden on Erev Pesach. Maharal states that if one has only matzah ashirah at the seder, he should eat it to at least fulfill one element of the mitzvah of matzah.

24. M.B. 471 §20; see also M.B. 444 §8, Shaar HaTziun ad loc. §1, and Responsa Yehudah Yaaleh 5.

D. Eating on Erev Pesach After the Tenth Hour

As previously noted one may not eat any bread, cake or the like (made from grain, even if not chametz) from the tenth hour and on.[25] One may eat fruits or vegetables after this time, but should be careful not to eat too much. This prohibition is designed to insure that one eat matzah at the seder with appetite and zest.[26]

E. Work on Erev Pesach

Erev Pesach from noon onwards has a quasi-festival status, which is reflected in the prohibition against doing many forms of work. *Yerushalmi*[27] explains that when the Temple stood, this was the time that every Jew had to offer the *pesach* sacrifice. Additionally, *Rashi*[28] explains that this work prohibition was enacted so that one not be distracted from his obligations to dispose of his chametz, offer the *pesach* sacrifice, and prepare his matzos. Since he is not allowed to work, he will finish these preparations in a timely fashion and be able to begin the seder immediately upon arriving home. Even in the post-Temple era this prohibition was continued.[29] Furthermore, as reported by the Mishnah, some localities extended the work prohibition to include the morning of Erev Pesach as well. Everyone must conform to the custom followed in his locality.[30] *Rama*[31] reports that the custom is to refrain from work in the morning, but later *poskim* assert that this custom is not universal.[32] In general, any work prohibited on *Chol HaMoed* is prohibited Erev Pesach after noon. Similarly,

---

25. *Pesachim* 99b.

26. O.C. 471:1.

27. *Pesachim* 4:1.

28. To *Pesachim* 50a.

29. Ibid.; O.C. 468:1.

30. *Pesachim* ibid.; O.C. 468:4.

31. O.C. 468:3.

32. M.B. ibid. §12.

all of the leniencies that apply to *Chol HaMoed* — e.g. work done to avert monetary loss — apply also to Erev Pesach.[33*]

F. Shacharis

In the time of the Temple, sacrifices had to be eaten within a prescribed period from the time of their having been offered. If that time allotment would have to be curtailed, the sacrifice would not be brought. Thus, the *todah* offering, which included *chametz* breads, was not brought on Erev Pesach since the Kohanim would not be allowed to eat the breads past midday. Therefore, *Mizmor L'Sodah*, said in commemoration of the *todah* offering, is omitted on Erev Pesach.[36]

Because of the quasi-festival nature of the day, *Keil Erech Apayim*, and *Lamenatzeiach* are omitted as well.[37**]

---

* When Erev Pesach Occurs on Shabbos:

The majority of *poskim* adopt the *Yerushalmi's* reason for the work prohibition on Erev Pesach. Accordingly, since in Temple times when Erev Pesach occured on Shabbos one would sacrifice the *pesach* offering on Shabbos, the work prohibition does not apply on Friday.[34]

Some *poskim* suggest adopting a more stringent view in accordance with *Rashi's* opinion, according to which the work prohibition *would* apply on Friday.[35]

❧ ❧ ❧

** *Mizmor L'Sodah* is recited on Friday[38] as is *Lamenatzeiach*.[39]

---

33. *O.C.* 468, M.B. §7. The details of what is and what is not permitted on *Chol HaMoed* are beyond the scope of this work.

34. See *Beur Halachah* 468:1 s.v. *m'chatzos v'eilech*. According to *Rashi's* reason, however, the Erev Pesach work prohibition *would* apply on Friday, since one must make all seder preparations before Shabbos.

35. See *Birkei Yosef* 468. *Beur Halachah* ibid. concludes: "*Perhaps* one need not adopt the stringent view."

36. *O.C.* 429:2, M.B. §12.

37. *O.C.* ibid.

38. *Chok Yisrael* §6. See *Magen Avraham* 429 §7 and *Machatzis HaShekel* ad loc. for explanation of why it is omitted on a regular Erev Pesach.

39. *Chok Yisrael* 66.

G. Hag'alas Keilim — Kashering

1. Preferably one should do all kashering for Pesach at least three days prior to Pesach.[40] This is to assure that it is done calmly and correctly.[41]
2. Generally, the latest time for kashering is Erev Pesach before the fifth hour.[42]*

H. Eruvei Chatzeiros

Biblically, it is permitted to carry on Shabbos within the confines of any reshus hayachid [enclosed area; lit: private domain] or between any contiguous reshus hayachid areas. The Rabbis, though, forbade carrying between reshuyos hayachid tenanted by different people (e.g. from a house into a common courtyard, or from one house into another), since it has the appearance of carrying from one domain to another. The Rabbis permitted, however, carrying between reshuyos hayachid if they have been merged through an eruvei chatzeiros. This eruv (a loaf of bread or matzah jointly owned by the various tenants and placed in one of the houses) symbolizes that the participating residents reside in the house in which they have left their eruv bread. As a result, all the houses and yards are viewed as the province of that one house (in which the various residents have been joined), rather than as distinct domains, and carrying is therefore permitted throughout.[44]

1. One may make the eruvei chatzeiros on any weekday, but not on Shabbos or Yom Tov.[45] However, it is customary to

---

* **When Erev Pesach Occurs on Shabbos:**

One may, if necessary, kasher on Friday even after midday.[43]

---

40. Maharil cited by Magen Avraham O.C. 452 §69.
41. Shiyurei Knesses HaGedolah, cited in Kaf HaChaim 452 §26.
42. O.C. 452:1.
43. See Chok Yisrael §15.
44. See Rashi to Eruvin 21b s.v. Shlomo tikken. Cf. Rambam, Hil. Eruvin 1:1.
45. Avodas HaKodesh, Shaar 4 Ch. 4:21, based on Shabbos 24a.

make the *eruv* for the *whole* year on Erev Pesach with matzah that may be eaten on Pesach.[46]*

I. Hafrashas Challah — Separation of Challah

The Torah commands (*Bamidbar* 15:17-21) that one separate a portion from dough kneaded for baking and give it to a Kohen. This portion is called *challah*. This Biblical directive applies only in the Land of Israel. In the diaspora, however, the obligation to separate *challah* is only Rabbinic.[48] If *challah* is not separated, the dough (or bread) may not be eaten.

---

* When Erev Pesach Occurs on Shabbos:

One must make the *eruvei chatzeiros* on Friday instead of on Erev Pesach itself.

Even if one is making an *eruvei chatzeiros* only for this Shabbos (which is Erev Pesach) and not for the entire year, it is preferable to use matzah rather than bread.[47]

---

46. *Darkei Moshe (Rama) O.C.* 366:1, quoting *Kol Bo*, explains that matzah (rather than bread) is generally used for the *eruvei chatzeiros* because the *eruv* is invalidated if it becomes inedible and matzah keeps much better than bread. *Rama* cites another reason: Since customarily only one *eruv* is made for the entire year, it must be edible all year long — even on Pesach. Hence, the *eruv* is made of matzah that is kosher for Pesach. See *O.C.* 368:5; *Rama* and *O.C.* 394:2.

47. For the *eruv* will then be effective even for the days of Yom Tov that follow. [Though carrying is anyway permitted on Yom Tov, that permit is limited to carrying *for Yom Tov needs*. An *eruv* will allow one to carry in the merged area unreservedly. And although an *eruv* cannot be made *just* for Yom Tov, one made for Shabbos permits carrying even on Yom Tov. (Preferably, one should *specify* when making the *eruv* that it function not only for Shabbos but for Yom Tov as well.) See *M.B.* 528:1.]

[Though the Rabbis forbade eating matzah on Erev Pesach (see VI:B), matzah is fit for use as an *eruv* on this Shabbos, since it is permitted to feed matzah to a young child on Erev Pesach (see *Rama* 471:2). Moreover, since it is permitted to eat the matzah *bein hashemashos* of Friday night, the *eruv* is valid for the entire Shabbos (see *Rama O.C.* 471:2 and *O.C.* 386:8). Furthermore, according to most authorities there is no prohibition to eat matzah on the night of Erev Pesach. (However, *Magen Avraham* 471:6 rules that this prohibition does begin at night. See *Igros Moshe O.C.* 1:155.)]

48. *Shulchan Aruch Yoreh Deah* 322:3.

The minimum amount of dough from which *challah* must be separated is the volume of 43.2 eggs.

Nowadays, since all people are presumed to be *t'mei mes* (contaminated with *tumah* conveyed by a human corpse), and hence all dough is *tamei*, we do not give the *challah* to a Kohen since *challah* that is *tamei* may not be eaten; instead, we burn it.[49]

While *challah* of the diaspora — even when *tamei* — may be consumed by a Kohen who is a minor or by an adult Kohen who has immersed himself in the *mikveh* (in order to be purified from *tumas keri*), the custom is, nevertheless, to burn such *challah*.[50]

One who baked bread and forgot to separate *challah* prior to Shabbos may nonetheless partake of it by leaving over some of the bread and separating part of it after Shabbos to serve as *challah*. [This option is available only outside the Land of Israel.[51]] The actual separation of *challah*, however, is forbidden on Shabbos.[52] The above applies to separating, on Yom Tov, *challah* for bread (or matzah) baked before Yom Tov. One may, however separate *challah* for bread or matzah kneaded and baked on Yom Tov.[53*]

---

* When Erev Pesach Occurs on Shabbos:

The option of leaving over some bread from which *challah* will be separated is not viable, since one may not keep chametz in his possession after the sixth hour. Accordingly most authorities rule that if one forgot to separate *challah* from his bread before this Shabbos, there is no way to rectify the situation, and the bread may not be eaten.[54] If this occurs, a competent halachic authority should be consulted.

Due to the unrectifiable problem of *challah* when Erev Pesach occurs on Shabbos, one (whose wife has baked bread for this Shabbos) is

---

49. Ibid. 4.

50. Ibid. 5.

51. *Rama O.C.* 506:3; *M.B.* §20.

52. See *Beitzah* 36b; *O.C.* ibid.

53. *O.C.* 506:3.

54. *Magen Avraham* 506 §8 cited in *Beur Halachah* 444 s.v. *l'tzorech Shabbos*. *Eliyahu Rabbah, Chok Yaakov, Chemed Moshe, Shulchan Aruch HaGraz, Derech Chaim* and *Chayei Adam* all concur.

* When Erev Pesach Occurs on Shabbos:

obligated on Erev Shabbos, just before dark, to inquire of his wife (by way of reminder) regarding the separation of *challah*.[55] This should be done early enough to allow for the separation (if necessary) but not so early as to cause neglect due to the feeling that there is ample time to do so "later."[56]

One who forgot to separate *challah* from chametz bread on Friday prior to Erev Pesach which occurs on Shabbos may do so during the *bein hashemashos* (twilight**) period of Friday. [This applies only in the diaspora and *only* on this Shabbos.][57]

Likewise, if one forgot to separate *challah* from Pesach matzos before this Shabbos, he may do so during the *bein hashemashos* period.[58]

Even if a woman lit candles on Erev Shabbos and thus accepted upon herself the sanctity of Shabbos, she may nonetheless separate *challah* until the end of *bein hashemashos*. She certainly did not mean her acceptance of Shabbos to prevent her from separating *challah*, and it is viewed as if her early acceptance of Shabbos was made with the specific stipulation that she be allowed to separate *challah*.[59]

It is preferable, however, that she have someone who has not yet accepted the sanctity of Shabbos separate *challah* on her behalf. The second party should recite the appropriate *berachah* and the woman on whose behalf *challah* has been separated should answer *Amen*.[60]

**The period between sunset and *tzeis hakochavim*.

---

55. Based on Mishnah *Shabbos* 2:7; see *Magen Avraham* 260 §3, M.B. ad loc. §13 citing Responsa *Knesses Yechezkel* 23 [103 printed in M.B. is an error].

56. *Rav* ad loc.

57. M.B. 261 §4.

58. M.B. ibid.

59. Responsa *Shoel U'Meishiv* Vol. 2:23, who gives other reasons to permit this. For an analogous situation see *Turei Zahav* O.C. 600 §2 and M.B. ad loc. §7.

60. Responsa *Shvus Yaakov* Vol. 3:19, based on *Rama* O.C. 261:1, who permits one Jew who has accepted the sanctity of Shabbos early to ask another Jew to perform *melachah* on his behalf. The woman fulfills her obligation to separate *challah* by means of *shlichus* (agency).

VII: Seder Preparations

The seder table should be fully prepared so that the seder may commence as soon as the men return from *davening*. This is done to assure that the children remain awake to participate in the seder.[1]*

---

* When Erev Pesach Occurs on Shabbos:

One must prepare on a weekday for Shabbos or Yom Tov; but one may not prepare on Shabbos for Yom Tov, or on Yom Tov for Shabbos.[2] Even preparations not involving any *melachah* are forbidden if they involve inconvenience and effort.[3]

Hence, when Erev Pesach occurs on Shabbos, since one may not prepare for the seder on Shabbos, all preparations that can be made on Friday must be made then.[4] **Thus, during years in which Erev Pesach occurs on Shabbos, all references to "Erev Pesach" and "Before Pesach" in this section should be understood as referring to Friday.** Under no circumstances may any seder preparations be made on Shabbos. See below. Preparations that one forgot to make on Friday or that must be done on *motzaei Shabbos* may not be done until after *tzeis hakochavim* (emergence of the stars).[5] Women who want to begin preparations must recite the following formula after *tzeis hakochavim*: בָּרוּךְ הַמַּבְדִּיל בֵּין קֹדֶשׁ לְקֹדֶשׁ, *Blessed is He Who separates between the holy and the holy*. Only then are they permitted to light candles and commence seder preparations.[6]

---

1. *O.C.* 472:1. This is the basis of the custom to provide children with goodies on Pesach eve (see *Pesachim* 108b-109a) as well as the custom of grabbing the *afikoman*.

2. *Rambam, Yom Tov* 1:19; *O.C.* 513:1; *M.B.* §1.

3. *Magen Avraham* 503:1; *M.B.* ad loc. 1; see *Machatzis HaShekel* ad loc. for examples of such preparations.

4. See *Maran R' Yosef Chaim Sonnenfeld*: "One who is able should prepare a separate table in a separate room for the seder, with couches [or cushions] for leaning, dishes, saltwater, and all of the other seder needs. In this fashion he can avoid all delay on *motzaei Shabbos* in beginning the seder. Alternatively, if one can eat his Shabbos meals outside of his home, he can fully prepare his home on Friday for the seder."

Regarding whether one may have a non-Jew make seder preparations on Shabbos, see *Daas Torah O.C.* 444:1.

5. See III: 4 regarding the definition of *tzeis hakochavim*.

6. If she inadvertently recited instead בָּרוּךְ הַמַּבְדִּיל בֵּין קֹדֶשׁ לְחוֹל, she must recite the proper formula. See XI:A8.

A. Zeroa and Beitzah — Shankbone and Egg

Shankbone

1. A roasted shankbone, to commemorate the *pesach* offering, is one of the items placed on the seder plate.[7] It must be roasted before Yom Tov.[8]

2. If one forgot to roast the shankbone before Yom Tov, it is permitted to do so on the seder night. However, one must be careful to eat it the next day before nightfall.[9]

Egg

3. An egg is placed on the seder plate as a commemoration of the *chagigah* (festival) offering. Some cook it[10] while others prepare it by roasting.[11] One may eat it at the seder whether cooked or roasted.[12] Hence, if one plans to eat it some time during the seder or first day of Tom Tov, he may cook or roast it at night. If, however, he intends to eat it only on the second day of Yom Tov, he *must* cook or roast it prior to Yom Tov. (Of course, if possible it should be prepared before Yom Tov.)

B. Maror — Bitter Herbs

Lettuce — Romaine Lettuce

1. Those who use lettuce or romaine lettuce for *maror* must carefully check each of the leaves[13] for insects before Yom

---

7. *O. C.* 473:4.

8. Even though roasting and cooking is permitted on Yom Tov, one should preferably not roast the shankbone on the seder night. Since we do not eat roast meat at the seder (see *O.C.* 476:1), the shankbone might remain uneaten until after the first day of Yom Tov, and it will emerge that one has cooked unnecessarily on Yom Tov. See *Darkei Moshe* 473:10, *Magen Avraham* 473 §8, *M.B.* ad loc. §32. See also *Maran R' Yosef Chaim Sonnenfeld* §4.

9. *O.C.* 473, *M.B.* §32. It may not be left over and eaten since cooking on the first day of Yom Tov for consumption on the second day (and certainly for weekday consumption) is forbidden. See *Shaar HaTziun* ad loc. §39. See fn. 8.

10. *O.C.* 473:4.

11. *Rama* ad loc.

12. *M.B.* ad loc. §32.

13. See *Kashrus HaMazon — Guide to Insect Checking*, for proper checking procedure. See also *Siddur Pesach K'Hilchaso* 1:4.

Tov. The leaves should also be checked to assure that they are not dried out or wilted.[14] After checking, one should place the leaves in the refrigerator so that they not wilt[15] or become infested with insects.[16]

If one does not have God-fearing individuals who can thoroughly check the leaves for insects, it is preferable to use horeseradish or *lettuce stalks* (which are easier to check) for the mitzvah of *maror*. Since consumption of insects entails transgression of many Biblical prohibitions, one may certainly not risk transgression in order to fulfill the Rabbinically mandated mitzvah of *maror*.[17]

2. One may not soak the leaves in water over a twenty-four hour period, since such prolonged soaking will disqualify them for use as *maror*.[18]

3. If one forgot to check the leaves before Yom Tov, they may be checked on Pesach. One must take caution to check only the maror for the first night, and not to transgress the *melachah* of *borer* (selecting). Hence if while checking one finds insects, he must remove a piece of leaf along with the insect. One may not wash the leaves with vinegar or salt water, since this kills the insects.[19]

Horseradish

4. Some have the custom to use horseradish for *maror*. When purchasing the *maror* one should ascertain that it was not cut with a chametz knife.[20]

---

14. See *Shemiras Shabbos K'Hilchasah* 3:36.

15. O.C. 473:5; M.B. §37 states that some authorities forbid the use of wilted leaves. *Luach Eretz Yisrael* (*HaRav Tukichinsky*) writes that one should follow the more stringent view.

16. *Siddur Pesach K'Hilchaso* ibid.

17. M.B. 473 §42.

18. O.C. 473:5 M.B. §38.

19. *Shemiras Shabbos K'Hilchasah* ibid. *Siddur Pesach K'Hilchaso* 9:3.

20. See *Haggadah Moadim U'Zmanim*. *Orchos Rabbeinu* cites this as the custom of the *Chazon Ish*.

5. Many authorities maintain that the horseradish is to be ground on Erev Yom Tov in order to allow some of the sharpness to dissipate.[21] If one forgot to do so, he should follow the procedure in the next paragraph.[22]*

Others are of the opinion that it is preferable to grind the horseradish used for *maror* on Yom Tov night, upon arriving at home for the seder.[24] The grinding should be done with a minor *shinui*.[25] One should grind only the approximate amount needed for *maror* and *korech* at the first seder. Horseradish needed for the second night must be ground on the second night of Yom Tov after

---

* **When Erev Pesach Occurs on Shabbos:**

The horseradish should be ground on Friday. It should be placed in a *sealed* receptacle until the beginning of the seder, in order to insure that it retain a sufficient degree of sharpness.[23]

---

21. M.B. 473 §36.

22. Grinding and chopping of items whose taste does not dissipate if ground before Yom Tov should not be done on Yom Tov (O.C. 504:1). Since one could have grated the horseradish before Yom Tov, he must now do so with a minor *shinui*. For example, it should be grated onto a table or tablecloth rather than into a utensil. See M.B. 504 §19. [The definition of *shinui* is different relative to each *melachah*.]

23. *Erev Pesach Shechal B' Shabbos* §13 of R' Moshe Sternbuch shlita. See *Orchos Rabbeinu*; See also *Luach Dvar Yom B'Yomo*.

24. *Chayei Adam* 130:3 (cited by M.B. ibid.) states: "The custom of the *Gra* was not to grind it [the *maror*] before returning from the *beis haknesses* in order that its [sharp] taste not dissipate. Were this to happen, one would not fulfill the mitzvah. Rather he should grind it after coming home and cover it until the beginning of the seder." *Kitzur Shulchan Aruch* 118:3 rules likewise.

25. *Kitzur Shulchan Aruch* ibid. [Though this is the ruling of the *Kitzur Shulchan Aruch*, the issue needs further study. As alluded to earlier, only items that can be ground on Erev Yom Tov need be ground with a minor *shinui* on Yom Tov (see M.B. 504 §19). Hence, *maror* for the seder, which according to these authorities *must* be ground on Yom Tov, should not require any *shinui*. Interestingly, when citing the *Gra*, M.B. 473 §36 (in spite of his opinion in 504 §19) makes no mention of any need for *shinui*. Furthermore, *Orchos Rabbeinu* reports that the custom of the *Chazon Ish* was to grind the horseradish on the seder night without employing any *shinui*. Nonetheless, the only explicit opinion on the matter is the *Kitzur Shulchan Aruch* cited.]

tzeis hakochavim.[26] The horseradish should be kept in a covered receptacle until the seder begins.[27]

C. Karpas

6. Preferably, one should prepare the vegetables for *karpas* on Erev Pesach. If one uses celery (or some similar vegetable) for *karpas,* any washing, checking for insects, or other preparations should be done on Erev Pesach.

D: Charoses, Saltwater, Seder Plate (Ke'arah)

Charoses

1. One should chop the *charoses* on Erev Pesach.[28] If one forgot to do so, he may chop it on the seder night with a minor *shinui.*[29]

2. Preferably, the wine should be poured into the *charoses* at the time one intends to use it for dipping the *maror.*[30] No *shinui* is necessary when doing so.[31]

Saltwater

3. It is preferable to prepare the saltwater for *karpas* on Erev Pesach.[32] If one forgot to do so, he may prepare it on the seder night,[33] but some authorities are of the opinion that one should then employ a *shinui* in preparing the saltwater (e.g. putting the water in the bowl first and then adding the salt if it is generally prepared in the reverse order).[34]

---

26. *Kitzur Shulchan Aruch* ibid.

27. *M.B.* 473 §36.

28. *Pri Megadim, Mishbetzos Zahav* 444:2.

29. See *O.C.* 504:1.

30. *Chayei Adam* 130:4; *Kitzur Shulchan Aruch* 118:4. See *Tosafos* to *Pesachim* 116a s.v. *tzarich l'asmuchai.*

31. *O.C.* 506:2. No *shinui* is necessary, since the *melachah* of *lishah* (kneading) is permitted on Yom Tov. Since the wine should be added at this time, the kneading could not have been done before Yom Tov.

32. *Chayei Adam* 130 in his *Concise Laws of the Seder* §1.

33. *Magen Avraham* 473:5; *M.B.* ad loc §21. See also *Maadanei Shmuel* 118 §13.

34. *Chayei Adam* and *Kitzur Shulchan Aruch* ibid.

Seder Plate

4. One should prepare the seder plate on Erev Yom Tov.[35]*

---

* When Erev Pesach Occurs on Shabbos:

Since preparation for the seder is forbidden on Shabbos,[36] when possible, one should prepare everything on Friday. The rest should be done on the *Seder* night.

Assorted Preparations

1. The wine for the four cups may not be prepared on Shabbos (such as by removing it from its case or placing it on the table).

2. Similarly, one may not carry wine for the seder from place to place (even through an *eruv*-enclosed area) on Shabbos.[37] If one will have difficulty getting wine after Shabbos, one may carry it to his home (through an *eruv*-enclosed area) under the following conditions: a) He brings it to his home while he is still permitted to partake of the wine during Shabbos itself,[38] and b) he carries it with some *shinui*.[39]

3. On this Shabbos, one may not take the matzos he needs for the seder to the place where it will be held (even through an *eruv*-enclosed area).[40]

4. On this Shabbos, one may not take the Haggadahs he needs to the seder location (even through an *eruv*-enclosed area). If it will otherwise be difficult to procure a Haggadah at night, one may be lenient and bring it on Shabbos provided that he studies from it during Shabbos.[41] Those who follow the custom of reading

---

35. *Chayei Adam* — *Concise Laws of the Seder* §1; O.C. 472:1.

36. Since one may not prepare on Shabbos for Yom Tov.

37. See M.B. 667 §5; *Chok Yisrael* 43.

38. See *Maran R' Yosef Chaim Sonnenfeld* §6 and *Beur Halachah* 471 s.v. *yayin me'at*.

39. M.B. ibid.

40. This would be preparation for Yom Tov on Shabbos. However, if one needs a Pesach matzah as a second "bread" for *lechem mishneh* at the Shabbos meal it is permissible to carry it through an *eruv*-enclosed area. Regarding whether Pesach matzoh is deemed *muktzeh* after the fifth hour (since at that time it is totally unusable) see *Aliba D'Hilchasa* p. 98 fn. 404.

41. Based on *Shaarei Teshuvah* O.C. 693 §1. *Aruch HaShulchan* 693:3 disagrees in the case of a *Megillah* under discussion there. In the case of the Haggadah, one may follow the opinion of *Shaarei Teshuvah*.

the Haggadah on this Shabbos (see I:C2) may transport the Haggadah for this purpose.

5. If one naps on this Shabbos, he should not say: "I am going to rest in order not to be tired at the seder."[42]

6. One should remember to bring the special Yom Tov *machzor* (prayerbook) to the synagogue before Shabbos. It is forbidden to bring it to the synagogue on Shabbos (even through an *eruv*-enclosed area) since this constitutes a preparation for Yom Tov.[43]

---

42. *Shemiras Shabbos K'Hilchasah* 28:72 states that one may *intend* to nap for that purpose, but he may not *articulate* that intent. This is equally true when instructing children to nap on this Shabbos. See, however, *Pri Megadim, Eishel Avraham O.C.* 307:1.

43. A *machzor* [unlike the Haggadah (see above #4)] has no function on Shabbos; carrying it, then, is clearly a preparation for Yom Tov, since his sole intent in bringing it to the synagogue on Shabbos is that he have it there on Yom Tov.

VIII: Seudos Shabbos — The Shabbos Meals

In order to design an approach to planning the Shabbos meals for Erev Pesach that occurs on Shabbos, it is necessary to understand some of the pertinent issues.

A. The Obligation of Three Shabbos Meals

One must eat three meals on Shabbos.[1] The Gemara[2] cites a Biblical verse as a source for this obligation: *Moses said, "Eat it today, for today is a Sabbath for Hashem; today you shall not find it [the manna] in the field."*[3]

There is a disagreement among the commentators regarding the exact status of this obligation. Some authorities accord this the status of Biblical obligation,[4] while others view the Biblical reference as a mere *asmachta* [an allusion found in Scripture for a Rabbinic enactment] and deem the obligation to eat three meals on Shabbos as one of Rabbinic origin.[5] Yet others cite the verse in *Isaiah: If you proclaim the Shabbos "a delight"*[6] as the source for this obligation.[7]

---

1. *Shabbos* 117b.

2. Ibid.

3. *Shemos* 16:25. The triple use of the word "today" is the source for the three meals. See *Shabbos* 118a: "One who fulfills the obligation of the three Shabbos meals will be saved from three calamities — the birth pains of the Mashiach, the judgment of purgatory and the war of Gog and Magog." See *Aruch HaShulchan* 291:1 regarding some of the deeper hidden reasons for the three meals. He concludes: "Great and awesome things are dependent upon these three meals as explained in many places in the *Zohar*."

4. *Teshuvos Min HaShamayim* 14, *Ran* in *Rif* Ch. II *Succah*, s.v. *Rabbi Eliezer omer;* Responsa of *Rashba* 614, cited in *Pri Megadim*, *Mishbetzos Zahav* §2; see Responsa of *Rashba* (formerly attributed to *Ramban*) 201, who compares the obligation of eating matzah on Pesach to the obligation of eating bread on Shabbos, "both of which were Scripturally established as an obligation." *Turei Zahav O.C.* 678 §2 and Responsa *Chasam Sofer O.C.* 46 concur. See *Beur Halachah* 288 s.v. *assur lihisanos.*

5. *M.B.* 291 §1; *Daas Torah O.C.* 274 §4; see *S'dei Chemed Maareches HaLamed* 27.

6. *Isaiah* 58:13.

7. Novellae of *Rashba* to *Berachos* 49b. See Responsa of *R' Akiva Eiger*, Vol. I Addenda 1.

In order to fulfill this obligation, one must eat bread[8] at all three meals,[9] though some are lenient and allow one to fulfill the third meal by eating cake, or even meat or fish, or even fruit.[10] Furthermore, one should break bread on *lechem mishneh* (two loaves of bread) for these meals.[11] Hence, one must have some type of bread to eat even on Erev Pesach that occurs on Shabbos.

The *Shulchan Aruch* rules that *seudah shlishis* (the third Shabbos meal) must be eaten after six and a half hours of the day have passed.[12] Some, however, rule that the obligation is fulfilled even if one eats it earlier.[13]

B. Retaining Chametz After Biur

The Talmud teaches that when Erev Pesach occurs on Shabbos, one may retain chametz food only as needed for two Shabbos meals.[14] This is predicated upon the custom in Talmudic times to dispose of the chametz immediately prior to the onset of Shabbos, when Shabbos coincides with Erev Pesach. However, according to our custom that even in such years we dispose of the chametz before midday, one may retain chametz food for consumption on the remainder of Friday, in addition to what he needs for the Shabbos meals.[15]

All chametz should be kept in a designated, well-guarded area. All housecleaning and kashering of kitchen and utensils must be completed before Shabbos. One must take care to clean the garbage bin of all chametz before Shabbos. One may not leave chametz in the garbage bin even if he places it outside on the street.[16]

---

8. *Shabbos* 117b; O.C. 274:1.
9. *S'mag* cited in *Beis Yosef* 291 s.v. *v'yesh omrim*. *Shulchan Aruch HaGraz* 274:5.
10. O.C. 291:5
11. O.C. 291:4.
12. O.C. 291:2.
13. See references cited in IX:D fn. 38.
14. *Pesachim* 13b.
15. *Beur Halachah* O.C. 444:1 s.v. *u'mesheirin mazon*.
16. *Igros Moshe* O.C. 3:57.

IX: Seudos Shabbos — Options

Based on the considerations outlined above, the Shabbos-meal menu may be designed in one of three ways:
(a) Pesach food with *lechem mishneh* of chametz;
(b) Pesach food with *lechem mishneh* of *matzah ashirah*;
(c) Regular chametz meal.

A. Pesach Food with Lechem Mishneh of Chametz[1]

1. Even though all the food served is kosher for Pesach, since chametz bread is eaten at this meal, one must use chametz or disposable utensils, etc.[2] It is preferable to use disposable items for this Shabbos rather than chametz utensils in order to simplify the cleanup process.[3]

2. One should be careful to eat the *lechem mishneh* bread in one place and not allow crumbs to be spread about.

3. Since Pesach pots are used in preparing this meal, one should be careful that all serving utensils and spices be kosher for Pesach.

4. Due to the many potential pitfalls one should — where possible — not use the Pesach pots in which he cooked this meal during the rest of Pesach.[4]

5. All foods served should contain absolutely no mixtures of chametz and should be cooked on the Pesach stove.

6. One must be careful not to remove food with a chametz spoon from the Pesach pot and not to pour boiling Pesach food into a chametz dish or pot.[5]

7. If one wants to pour piping hot Pesach food from a Pesach pot into a chametz dish,[6] he should wait until the food

---

1. Based on *Maran R' Yosef Chaim Sonnenfeld* §3.
2. *Pri Chadash O.C.* 444 §3.
3. *Luach Ezras Torah* of *R' Yosef Eliyahu Henkin zt"l.*
4. See *Maran R' Yosef Chaim Sonnenfeld* ibid.
5. *Shaar HaTziun* 444 §4 citing *Pri Megadim, Aishel Avraham* §4.
6. See *M.B.* 318 §87. See *Badei HaShulchan Y.D.* 92:9 *Beurim* s.v. *aval cheilev.*

cools down (or pour the food into a Pesach *kli sheini**), and then pour it into a chametz vessel.[8] Care should be taken that the chametz and Pesach vessels do not touch each other.[9]

8. If one inadvertently poured boiling food from a Pesach vessel to a chametz vessel, the Pesach vessel does not become forbidden for Pesach use.[10]

9. One who handles chametz should be careful not to touch any Pesach pots or serving utensils without first cleaning his hands. Likewise, one should remove all crumbs from his face and clothes before touching Pesach vessels.

10. Some authorities suggest an alternative option in order to avoid many of the potential pitfalls: One should eat a meal of cold food with bread in the morning after *kiddush*, remove all chametz items before the fifth hour, and have a warm Pesach meal after midday.[11]

[A variation of the above option has been suggested by contemporary *poskim*.[12]

(a) One may dispose of all chametz (except for the *lechem mishneh* bread,[13]) and pack away all chametz utensils and items in the chametz area on Friday. On this Shabbos he will use only Pesach utensils and Pesach food as if it were already Yom Tov.

---

* A *kli sheini* is a vessel that is not the original vessel in which the hot food was cooked, but rather the vessel into which the hot food or liquid was poured. Many do *not* consider a ladle dipped into the cooking pot to be a *kli sheini*.[7]

---

7. See fn. 6.

8. *Pri Megadim*, ibid. citing *Pri Chadash* 444 §3; *Ohr Yisrael* 444:3.

9. Based on *Chochmas Adam* 74:4.

10. *Pri Megadim* ibid. See *Rama Yoreh Deah* 105:3 who rules that *nitzuk* (a continuous flow) is not deemed connected to prohibit the use of the vessel from which one poured. See also *Yad Yehudah* 95 in his extensive commentary §28, and *Badei HaShulchan* ibid. §73.

11. M.B. 444 §14. See *Collected Letters of Chazon Ish* 1:188.

12. This variation is found in the digest of laws for Erev Pesach of the *beis din* of *Hisachdus HaRabbanim*. See also *Hilchos Erev Pesach Shechal B'Shabbos* of *Rabbi Shimon Eider shlita*.

13. One may use a Pesach matzah as the second loaf of *lechem mishneh*. See below, 12.

(b) After making *kiddush*, one washes and eats more than a *k'beitzah*[14] (egg volume) of the *lechem mishneh* bread using a separate (non-Pesach) tablecloth. After finishing the bread, he should clean the crumbs from the tablecloth, his person, and the area he ate in, and flush them down the toilet.

(c) One should then thoroughly wash his hand and mouth, and clean his teeth of all chametz. (See below, 11 through 20.)

(d) One may then set out a Pesach tablecloth and continue the meal using only Pesach utensils and food. (No additional *berachos* are recited on the food; see below, 13.)]

11. One must finish eating chametz during the Shabbos morning meal before the fifth hour. Hence, *Shacharis* should be scheduled early and not be unduly prolonged.[15]

12. As previously explained, one should leave only a minimal amount of chametz for Shabbos use. However, one must be sure to fulfill the obligation of *lechem mishneh* (breaking bread on two loaves). One may use even a Pesach matzah as the second loaf of *lechem mishneh*.[16] (Obviously he may not eat the Pesach matzah.) If one wants to use this matzah on Pesach, he should keep the matzah in a closed bag or the like when he holds it together with the chametz loaf for *lechem mishneh*.[17]

---

14. One may not recite the *al netilas yadaim* over washing unless he intends to eat a *k'beitzah*. See O.C. 155:2.

15. *Pri Chadash* 444 §1; *Ohr Yisrael* ad loc.; *Chok Yisrael* §24.

16. *Chazon Ish* ibid. Responsa *Pri HaSadeh* 88. Regarding whether Pesach matzah is considered *muktzeh* on Erev Pesach which occurs on Shabbos, see *Pri Megadim*, *Aishel Avraham* 444 §1, who writes that only matzah which may be fed to minors is not deemed *muktzeh*. According to *Chazon Ish*, however, even matzah that may be used at the seder is not *muktzeh*, since one may use it for *lechem mishneh*. After the fifth hour, however, when it may no longer be used for *lechem mishneh*, it seemingly would become *muktzeh*. See *Daas Torah*, glosses 444 s.v. *gam yeish lha'ir*. See also *Kaf HaChaim* 471 §24.

17. See *Orchos Rabbeinu* who cites this as the custom of the *Steipler Gaon*. See also *Shearim HaMetzuyanim B'Halachah* 115:6.

13. Upon arrival of the fifth hour (when one may no longer eat bread), one does not need to recite *Bircas HaMazon* or *berachos* on any of the remaining food. He may simply continue his meal eating Pesach food, and recite *Bircas HaMazon* at the conclusion of the meal.[18]

14. All utensils and dishes (disposable or chametz) used during this meal must be cleaned of chametz, and the chametz residue should be flushed down the toilet. The chametz utensils and dishes must be put away among the rest of one's chametz items before the end of the fifth hour.[19] One should shake off all crumbs from his person and clothes,* checking his pockets and hems for chametz.[20] One should rinse his mouth and clean his teeth after the meal. [Care must be taken not to make the gums bleed.[21]] All chametz crumbs etc. should be shaken out of the tablecloth into the toilet and flushed down.[22] The tablecloth should also be placed among one's chametz items. One should sweep the area over which he ate the chametz bread. If a broom was used for this cleaning it must be cleaned of chametz (and the chametz flushed down the toilet) and placed among one's chametz items. [A straw broom may not be used on *any* Shabbos.[23]] One may not put chametz in a garbage can even if it will be placed in the public domain enclosed within an *eruv*.[24]

Since one will need to remove the tablecloth to shake out the chametz crumbs, one should take care on Friday not to place the Shabbos candlesticks on the tablecloth he intends to use for eating the *lechem mishneh* of chametz.[25]

---

* Care must be taken to clean the clothes in a fashion permitted on Shabbos.

---

18. See *Aliba D'Hilchasa* p. 99 fn. 407.
19. O.C. 444:4; M.B. 444 §21.
20. M.B. 433 §47.
21. *Orchos Chaim* 433 §15.
22. M.B. 444 §21.
23. M.B. O.C. 337 §14, *Beur Halachah* s.v. *shelo yishtabru*.
24. *Igros Moshe* O.C. 3:57.
25. *Hilchos Erev Pesach Shechal B'Shabbos* of Rabbi Shimon Eider shlita.

15. If one must wash any utensils or dishes from this meal, he should not use the kitchen sink, since it is kosher for Pesach. Rather, the bathroom sink should be used and then rinsed thoroughly.

    One may not use the hot water to wash these dishes since this entails chilul Shabbos (desecration of Shabbos).

16. All materials needed for covering counters, shelves, as well as any other items needed for final Pesach preparations should be torn, cut and prepared before Shabbos. Tearing them on Shabbos is of course forbidden.

17. One who wears dentures should wash them thoroughly after the meal. In addition, some authorities suggest that one kasher them before Shabbos, and then (on Shabbos) eat chametz food only if it is cooler than yad soledes (between 110° and 160°F; 43° and 71° C*).[26]

18. All remaining chametz must be disposed of before the end of the fifth hour. The bitul formula must be recited at that time.

19. If one has in his possession a considerable amount of chametz and has not arranged for its sale, a competent halachic authority should be consulted.

20. As previously explained, one may not derive any benefit from chametz after the sixth hour. Furthermore, on this Shabbos chametz becomes muktzeh [forbidden for handling] at that time. Hence, if one found chametz after the sixth hour he may not move it, have his animal eat it or have a non-Jew take it as a gift. He may, however, ask the non-Jew to flush it down the toilet for him. Alternatively, he should cover it over until Chol HaMoed, at which time it should be burned.[27]

---

* This definition of yad soledes is reported in the name of HaGaon R' Moshe Feinstein zt"l.

---

26. Responsa Maharsham suggests kashering by pouring boiling water from a kli rishon. [Responsa Minchas Yitzchak 8:37 permits this even on Shabbos.] Responsa Shevet HaLevi permits even hot water from a kli sheini. See Responsa Tzitz Eliezer 9:25 for opinions regarding this matter. Orchos Rabbeinu reports Chazon Ish's opinion that dentures need not be kashered.

27. M.B. 444 §21.

B. Pesach Food with Lechem Mishneh of Matzah Ashirah

Beis Yosef, after delineating the problematic issues involved in planning the Shabbos meals when Erev Pesach occurs on Shabbos, concludes: "Do not ask: Why not dispose of *all* chametz before Shabbos and eat *matzah ashirah* on Shabbos? Since not everyone is able to prepare *matzah ashirah* for all three Shabbos meals, the Sages did not obligate one to do so."[28]

This implies that if the *matzah ashirah* option was available, it would be preferable. Since according to most authorities one may eat *matzah ashirah* until the fifth hour on Erev Pesach, this is the preferred option, particularly in situations where it is difficult to assure that no chametz is spread about (e.g. where there are young children or elderly parents present).[29]

1. All chametz and chametz utensils should be disposed of before Shabbos, as if it were in fact Erev Pesach.

   [Unlike those who retain chametz for Shabbos, one using this option should recite the *bitul* formula on Friday at the time of burning chametz and repeat it on Shabbos (see IV:A4).]

2. All foods and utensils used for this Shabbos should be kosher for Pesach.

3. One should wash as for bread and use *matzah ashirah* for *lechem mishneh*. Since one is using it as bread *along with the other foodstuffs generally eaten at a dinner meal* he recites *hamotzi* on the *matzah ashirah*.[30] Other authorities mandate

---

28. O.C. 444 s.v. *v'chein hinhig Rashi.*

29. See *Noda B'Yehudah* O.C. Vol. 1:21 who writes: "If not for the foremost of authorities, *Rama,* who prohibits eating *matzah ashirah* on Erev Pesach, I would permit eating it the entire day (i.e even for *seudah shlishis*). At any rate, I rule that even *Rama* would permit eating *matzah ashirah* until midday." He cites *Magen Avraham* 443 §2 and interprets his words to indicate that one may use *matzah ashirah* for the first two Shabbos meals. See also *Igros Moshe* ibid. and Responsa *Yechaveh Daas* 91 who cites many authorities who advised this option. [According to the *Gra,* however, who forbids the use of *matzah ashirah* from Erev Pesach morning (see VI:C), this is not a viable option.]

30. *M.B.* 168 §24 and *Igros Moshe* O.C. 3:32.
   According to R' Shlomo Zalman Auerbach *shlita,* in order to consider this amount as a *seudah* one should eat some of the other foods (e.g. meat or fish) along with

reciting *hamotzi* on the *matzah ashirah* even if it is consumed wth less than a normal meal since it functions as an *obligatory* Shabbos *seudah*.[31]

4. One may not eat *matzah ashirah* after the fifth hour.[32] At that time, one may continue eating all the kosher for Pesach foods. He need not recite *Bircas HaMazon* at that time nor need he recite any *berachos* before partaking of the Pesach foodstuff.[33]

C. Regular Chametz Meal

If one has a special Pesach kitchen and can cook chametz meals for this Shabbos, he may do so. He must take care to place all chametz in a secure location so as to assure that it not be spread about.[34]

1. One should not cook any kugel or cereal-like foods which tend to stick to pots or dishes.[35] Cleaning these dishes from the sticky residue is forbidden on this Shabbos. Since one has no use for these chametz pots or dishes, cleaning them is considered preparation on Shabbos for a weekday and is prohibited.

2. If one inadvertently cooked such a sticky type dish he may remove the residue with his fingers.[36] If this is impossible, he may have a non-Jew wash it out. If this, too, is not possible, one may lightly wash the dirty dishes and pots — enough to remove the chametz residue.[37]

3. Chametz items stored in a refrigerator that will be used for Pesach should preferably be kept on a separate shelf. One

---

the *matzah ashirah* [rather than finishing the *matzah ashira* and then beginning to eat the other foods]; otherwise it may be necessary to eat a much larger amount of *matzah ashira* in order for this to be deemed a *seudah* and for one to be allowed to recite *bircas hamazon*.

31. *Igros Moshe O.C.* 1:155.

32. *Shulchan Aruch HaGraz* 444:3; *Igros Moshe* ibid. See fn. 29.

33. See fn. 18.

34. *O.C.* 434:1

35. *O.C.* 444:3; *M.B.* §11.

36. *Rama* ad loc.; see *M.B.* §14.

37. Ibid.

must take great care that the chametz and Pesach items in the refrigerator remain separate.

See Section A:11-20 for further instructions.

D. Instructions for After the Meal

1. One should preferably divide the morning meal into two parts in order to fulfill the mitzvah of the third Shabbos meal with bread.[38] This should be done in the following fashion:[39]

    (a) Make *kiddush*, wash, make *hamotzi*, eat the meal, recite *Bircas HaMazon*.

    (b) One should recess for at least one-half hour.

    (c) A second meal (with washing, *hamotzi*, etc., and *Bircas HaMazon*) should be eaten.

    (d) All chametz or *matzah ashirah* must be eaten before the fifth hour.

2. The *bitul* formula must be recited before the end of the fifth hour.[40]

X: Seudah Shlishis — The Third Meal

A. Time

As previously explained,[1] one must eat three meals on Shabbos.[2] The third meal is to be eaten after six and one-half hours. If one eats it before this time he has not fulfilled the obligation.[3] The

---

38. Since according to some opinions, one may fulfill the obligation of *seudah shlishis* even before six and one-half hours. See *Magen Avraham* §1, *Beur HaGra* ad loc., M.B. ad loc. §8. See also *Chazon Ish* cited in X:3 fn. 13.

39. *Chazon Ish* ibid.

40. *M.B.* 444 §22.

1. See VIII:A.

2. See M.B. 291 §1: "Even a poor man must be provided with all three meals, as explained in [the laws of *tzedakah*] *Yoreh Deah* 250."

3. O.C. 291:2; see *Tosafos* to Shabbos 118a s.v. *b'minchah*. Responsa of *Rashba* (formerly attributed to *Ramban*) bases this on Shabbos 118a: "Eating utensils used on Friday night may be washed in order to eat from them at the morning meal; those of the morning meal may be washed for the afternoon meal; *those of the afternoon meal may be washed in order to eat from them at Minchah*. (See *Teshuvos Min*

prevalent and preferable custom is to pray the *Minchah* service before eating the third meal.[4] Woman, too, are obligated to eat *seudah shlishis*.[5]

B. Menu

As previously mentioned, one should preferably eat bread (or *matzah ashirah*) and have *lechem mishneh* even for *seudah shlishis*.[6] If this is impossible, one may use items made of the five grains whose *berachah* is *borei minei mezonos*. Others are of the opinion that meat or fish are sufficient for *seudah shlishis*, while yet other opinions permit even fruits. If one is satiated and finds it difficult to eat bread at this time, he may rely on the other opinions.[7]

Since one must eat the third meal after six and one-half hours, at which time both chametz and matzah are forbidden,[8] how can one fulfill the obligation of eating the third meal?

1. According to those authorities who permit eating *matzah ashirah* on Pesach, one may use *matzah ashirah* for *seudah shlishis*.[9] However, Ashkenazic custom[10] forbids eating *matzah ashirah* from the end of the fifth hour on Erev Pesach.

2. According to those who permit eating *kneidlach* (matzah balls) on Erev Pesach, one may eat them for *seudah shlishis*.[11] This must be done before the tenth hour of the

---

HaShamayim 14.) The *Arizal's* poem *Bnei Heichala* recited at *seudah shlishis* would seem likewise to indicate this time: *"Arei hashta b'minchasa — I ask now, at Minchah time."* [See, however, IX:D fn. 38.]

4. *Rama* ad loc.

5. O.C. ibid. 6.

6. O.C. ibid. 4; *M.B.* 291 §22 writes that it is proper to serve additional dishes according to one's financial ability.

7. O.C. ibid. 5.

8. See VI:B and C.

9. O.C. 444:1.

10. See *Rama* ad loc. *Kaf HaChaim* 444 §15 writes that even among Sephardim many have the custom not to eat *matzah ashirah* on Pesach.

11. *Pri Megadim, Eishel Avraham* 471 §8; *M.B.* 444 §8; *Chok Yisrael* §37. See also *Maharsham* glosses ad loc. for an extensive discussion of the matter. Regarding the use of matzah-meal *latkes* (*chremzlach*) or matzah-meal cake, see O.C. 444 *Shaar HaTziun* §1.

day.[12] (Of course, those who do not eat *gebrokts* may not use this option.)

3. According to those who forbid the use of *kneidlach* one may fulfill the obligation with meat and fish.[13] If this is not viable,[14] one may follow the lenient opinion and use fruits. See IX:D regarding dividing the morning meal in two.

Mishnah Berurah concludes the discussion with the following: "Presently the custom in many communities in our country is to eat a cold meal of chametz after the [morning] prayers, and after midday to eat a Pesach meal [without any bread or *matzah ashirah*] of foods which were cooked in Pesach pots and kept warm on the stove. In this fashion one can fulfill the obligation of *seudah shlishis*."[15]

XI: Motzaei Shabbos

A. Havdalah

1. When Yom Tov occurs on *motzaei Shabbos* we recite *Vatodi'einu* [וַתּוֹדִיעֵנוּ]. If one omitted this prayer he need not repeat *Shemoneh Esrei*.[1]

---

12. See VI:D.

13. This would seem to be the opinion of the *Gra*. See *Shaar HaTziun* ibid. See also Responsa *Yehudah Yaaleh* 65. *Chazon Ish* writes (*Collected Letters* Vol. I 188): "In the morning eat cold food: milk, cheese, eggs, fruit, or fruit juice, recite *Bircas HaMazon*, recess for one-half hour and then [wash] eat a *kezayis* of bread with fruit juice or the like. One should finish by 8:30 [according to the time in Israel]. After *Minchah* one should eat meat, fish and some Pesach dish." (See IX:D fn. 38 for explanation of dividing the morning meal and nonetheless eating *seudah shlishis* again in the afternoon.) *Rama* 444:1 speaks of eating fruit, meat or fish in the afternoon rather than any of the other *seudah shlishis* menu options. See *Magen Avraham* ad loc. §2. See Responsa *Minchas Yitzchak* 8:37 for extensive discussion of this matter.

14. M.B. 291 §8 writes that meat or fish are preferable to fruits.

15. M.B. 444 §14. *Magen Avraham* writes in the name of *Shelah*: "R' Shimon bar Yochai learned Torah instead of eating *seudah shlishis*. *Chasam Sofer* (novellae to *Pesachim*, in appendix to O.C. 444) writes that one who has no food for *seudah shlishis* may rely on this opinion.

1. O.C. 491:2; M.B. §4.

There is extensive debate in the Talmud[2] regarding the proper order in which to recite the elements of *Havdalah* and *Kiddush* when Yom Tov occurs on *motzaei Shabbos*.

The opinion of Rava is expressed in the mnemonic יקנה"ז, *YaKNaHaZ: Yayin* (wine); **Kiddush**; *Ner* (candle); *Havdalah; Z'man* (*Shehecheyanu* blessing). *Besamim* (spices) are not used for *Havdalah* when Yom Tov falls on *motzaei Shabbos*.[3]

2. *Kiddush* at the seder is recited as follows:[4] *Borei Pri HaGafen; Kiddush* — *Asher Bachar Banu* etc.; *Borei Meorei HaAish;*[5] *Baruch ... HaMavdil Bein Kodesh L'Chol* etc., with the ending *Baruch ... HaMavdil Bein Kodesh L'Kodesh;* and finally *Shehecheyanu*.

3. If one recited these blessings out of order, he need not repeat them. However, if he recited *Kiddush* before *Borei Pri HaGafen*, he must repeat the *Kiddush* blessing.[6]

---

2. See *Pesachim* 102b-103a for the different opinions and reasons.

3. *Rashbam* explains that one possesses a *neshamah yeseirah* (lit: extra soul) on Yom Tov. Since *besamim* are used on *motzaei Shabbos* to revive one from the loss of the *neshamah yeseirah*, there is no need for them on Yom Tov. *Tosafos* ibid. (s.v. *Rav amar*) explain that the absence of *besamim* is due to the extra food and drink of Yom Tov fulfilling the restorative function of *besamim*. *Shibbolei HaLeket* (*Pesach* 218) writes another reason — "out of fear one may pick the *besamim* spices on Yom Tov," an act which is prohibited. See *Tosafos* to *Beitzah* 33b (s.v. *ki havinan*).

4. *O.C.* 473:1.

5. Two candles of the Yom Tov candles should be held together with the flames touching (*Yesod V'Shoresh HaAvodah* 9:4, cited in *Alef HaMagen* 600 §53). *Yom Tov Sheini K'Hilchaso* 1 fn. 53 cites this as the opinion of *HaGaon R' Yosef Shalom Eliyashiv shlita*, along with a warning to be careful not to *attach* the candles for this would entail the *melachah* of *memachek* (smoothing). He further cites *HaGaon R' Shlomo Zalman Auerbach shlita* that one should not even have the flames touch. Any closer contact may precipitate transgression of *gram kibui* (causing extinguishing), which is forbidden on Yom Tov. *Likutei Te'amim U'Minhagim*, appended to *Shulchan Aruch HaGraz*, rules that two candles be held separately. See fn. 6 regarding if one recited *Borei Me'or* [rather than the proper *Meorei HaEish*].

6. *Shulchan Aruch HaGraz O.C.* 473:6. The order of reciting *Borei Pri HaGafen* and the *Kiddush* is debated in *Pesachim* 114a. Beis Hillel hold that *HaGafen* precedes *Kiddush*. Beis Shammai hold that *Kiddush* precedes *HaGafen*. The *halachah* follows Beis Hillel. One who follows Beis Shammai against the opinion of Beis Hillel does not (even *post facto*) fulfill his obligation. *Magen Avraham* 298 §3, citing *Bach*, rules that

4. If one forgot and did not recite *Havdalah* over the cup of *Kiddush*, he should continue with the recitation of the Hagaddah and recite *Havdalah* over the second of the four cups.[7] The order of recitation in that case is *HaGafen, Borei Meorei HaEish,* and *HaMavdil.*

5. If one realized that he had omitted *Havdalah* only after drinking the second cup, he must immediately (even during the meal) recite *Havdalah* over a cup of wine. However, he does not recite *Borei Pri HaGafen,* since its recitation before the meal absolves him from reciting a *berachah* on any wine (or drinks) during the meal. If when reciting the *Borei Pri HaGafen* he intended not to drink during the meal, he must recite *Borei Pri HaGafen* when making *Havdalah.*[8] The other elements of *Havdalah* are recited in the previously mentioned order (see 4 above).

6. If he realized during *Bircas HaMazon,* he recites *Havdalah* over the cup of *Bircas HaMazon,* following the previously mentioned order.[9] If one realized only after drinking the cup of *Bircas HaMazon,* he recites *Havdalah* over the fourth cup at the end of *Hallel.*[10]

7. If one forgot about *Havdalah* until after the fourth cup, he must recite it over a fifth cup. Even if he has not yet recited *Al HaGefen* (the *berachah* recited after drinking wine), he must recite a new *Borei Pri HaGafen* on this cup of *Havdalah.*[11]

---

one who recited *Borei Meor HaEish* (following Beis Shammai [*Berachos* 51b]) rather than *Borei Meorei HaEish* (following Beis Hillel) must repeat the blessing. *M.B.* ibid. §2 rules likewise. See *Tehillah L'David* 271 §15.

7. *O.C.* 473:1, *M.B.* §4, *Beur Halachah* s.v. *ad sheyaschil.* See *Shulchan Aruch HaGraz* ibid. 7 and Haggadah of *R' Moshe Sternbuch shlita,* who discuss the question of one who realized, before eating *karpas,* that he did not recite *Havdalah. Beur Halachah,* after citing *Shulchan Aruch HaGraz,* leaves the question unresolved.

8. *M.B.* 473:1 §5. See *Shaar HaTziun* §15; see *O.C.* 206:5, *M.B.* §20 and *Shaar HaTziun* §20.

9. Ibid.

10. Ibid. He may not recite *Havdalah* immediately upon remembering, since one may not drink additional cups of wine between the third and fourth cups (see *O.C.* 479:1).

11. Ibid.

8. One who concluded the *Havdalah* with הַמַּבְדִּיל בֵּין קֹדֶשׁ לְחוֹל, *HaMavdil Bein Kodesh L'Chol*, instead of הַמַּבְדִּיל בֵּין קֹדֶשׁ לְקֹדֶשׁ, *Hamavdil Bein Kodesh L'Kodesh* — and he did not correct himself[12] immediately* — must repeat *Havdalah*. He repeats *only* the *Havdalah* element; he does *not* repeat *Borei Meorei HaEish* or *Borei Pri HaGafen* [if he can still drink wine by virtue of the *Borei Pri HaGafen* he has already recited].

B. Asher Ge'alanu

1. Some authorities hold that when the seder is held on *motzaei Shabbos*, one should invert the text of the *Asher Ge'alanu berachah* as follows: וְנֹאכַל שָׁם מִן הַפְּסָחִים וּמִן הַזְּבָחִים.[13] Others disagree.[14] *Chazon Ish* followed the latter opinion.[15]

* "Immediately" is defined as *toch kdei dibur* — the amount of time it takes for a student to greet his teacher (usually reckoned as approximately 1 1/2 seconds).

---

12. See *Shemiras Shabbos K'Hilchasah* 62:21.

13. *Shaar HaTziun* 473 §80. [The usual order is מִן הַזְּבָחִים וּמִן הַפְּסָחִים, since *zevachim* is a reference to the *chagigah* offering, which was eaten before the *pesach* offering. When Erev Pesach coincided with Shabbos, however, no *chagigah* offering was brought that day. Hence, we invert the order.]

14. Responsa *Knesses Yechezkel*, cited in *Shaar HaTziun* ibid. [Those who disagree maintain that since this blessing is a prayer for the restoration of the Temple, where we will hopefully celebrate Pesach *next year* in complete fashion — with the *chagigah* and *pesach* sacrifices — there is no need to invert the order, because Erev Pesach will not fall *next year* on Shabbos.]

15. Cited in *Orchos Rabbeinu*.

⊷ Chronological Step by Step Checklist for Erev Pesach Which Occurs on Shabbos

THURSDAY MORNING:

☐ Fast of the Firstborn — Attendance at *siyum* or *seudas mitzvah* absolves one from this fast. P. 138.

☐ *Mechiras Chametz* must be arranged. P. 137.

THURSDAY EVENING:

☐ *Bedikas Chametz* followed by *bitul* formula; place remaining chametz in secure location. P. 125, 129, 135.

FRIDAY MORNING:

☐ Recite *Mizmor L'Sodah* and *Lamenatze'ach* at *Shacharis*. P. 146.

☐ *Biur Chametz* of all chametz not needed for Shabbos must be conducted before the end of the fifth hour. P. 136.

☐ The *bitul* formula is not recited. However, one who will retain no chametz into Shabbos should recite the *bitul* formula. P. 135.

☐ *Hafrashas Challah* (separation of *challah*) of both Pesach matzah and chametz bread must be arranged. P. 148.

☐ *Eruvei Chatzeiros* must be made. P. 147.

☐ Work is permitted Friday afternoon. Some refrain. P. 145.

☐ Kashering is permitted (when necessary) even after midday, but must be completed before Shabbos. P. 147.

☐ All chametz and chametz vessels not needed for Shabbos should be placed in the sealed chametz area. P. 161.

☐ All covering materials must be cut before Shabbos. Prepare twine or child-safety locks to reclose chametz closet and cupboards. P. 164.

☐ Care should be taken *not* to place the Shabbos candlesticks on top of the tablecloth on which one will eat chametz. P. 163.

Seder preparations: P. 151.

☐ The shankbone should be roasted before Shabbos. P. 152.

☐ The egg should be prepared before Shabbos. P. 152.

☐ Lettuce or romaine lettuce should be checked before Shabbos. P. 152.

☐ *Charoses* should be ground or chopped before Shabbos. P. 155.

☐ Saltwater should be prepared before Shabbos. P. 155.

☐ According to some authorities horseradish (used for *maror*) should be ground before Shabbos and placed in a sealed receptacle. P. 153.

☐ The *seder* plate (*ke'arah*) should be arranged before Shabbos. P. 156.

☐ All seals on wine bottles and matzah boxes needed for the seder should be opened.

SHABBOS MEAL PREPARATIONS:

☐ Purchase sufficient (but not more than necessary) *challah* or egg matzah for the Shabbos meals. If necessary one may make use of (but not eat) a matzah as the second of the *lechem mishneh*. P. 160.

☐ If possible purchase sufficient disposable dishes, utensils and table-cloths to avoid kashrus problems with chametz dishes or cleanup problems with Pesach dishes. P. 160.

☐ A chametz broom should be available for cleanup after the morning meal. P. 163.

FRIDAY NIGHT MEAL:

☐ The meals should be held in a room with a floor that may be swept on Shabbos. If the room is carpeted, a drop cloth or disposable tablecloth should be spread on the floor of the area where chametz will be eaten. The table should be covered with two new or disposable tablecloths. The *challos* should be on the table in a closed bag. [Regarding the use of egg matzos see P. 165.] P. 160.

☐ *Kiddush* should be made with a Pesach wine cup. All cups and wine bottles should be kosher for Pesach. All Pesach items must be removed from the table before cutting the *challos*. P. 160.

☐ One must wash and make *hamotzi* on *lechem mishneh* and eat at least a *k'beitzah* of *challah*. In order to facilitate crumb disposal it is prudent for each individual to eat the *challah* over a spread paper napkin. The napkin and crumbs should then be discarded into the toilet. P. 162.

☐ The top tablecloth and the drop cloth on the floor (after cleaning them of crumbs and discarding the crumbs into the toilet) are put away for use at the Shabbos morning meal or else discarded. P. 163.

☐ One must clean his face and hands of crumbs and rinse his mouth thoroughly. This should be done in the bathroom and not over the Kosher for Pesach sink. When leaving the bathroom one should wash his hands in the same fashion as for *netilas yadaim,* but *without* reciting the *berachah.* P. 162.

☐ The Shabbos meal is now eaten with Pesach food and utensils. [Disposable plates and utensils may be used. They should be of a quality befitting the honor of Shabbos.] P. 160.

☐ One may alternatively use *matzah ashirah* (egg matzah) for this meal. He must wash, make *hamotzi* and eat a *k'beitzah* of *matzah ashirah,* preferably eating it along with the food of the *seudah.* [The first five items listed above are not applicable when using *matzah ashirah.*]
If using Pesach food and chametz dishes see P. 160.

SHABBOS MORNING:

☐ *Shacharis* is scheduled earlier than usual to allow the completion of the meal and the removal and disposal of the chametz in a timely fashion. P. 158.

☐ One conducts the Shabbos morning meal following the first six items of the Friday night meal. After reciting *Bircas HaMazon* he recesses for one-half hour and then follows the third through fifth items.
Note: If one employs the *matzah ashirah* option he must divide his meal in two by reciting *Bircas HaMazon,* recessing for one half hour and repeating item 7.

☐ All leftover chametz must be disposed of into the toilet before the end of the fifth hour. The area around the table should be swept with a chametz broom and the crumbs thrown into the toilet. Alternatively, the drop cloth placed on the floor is removed and the crumbs on it discarded into the toilet. P. 159.
Note: All chametz items (broom, etc.) should be placed in the chametz closet. [Taping or tying with string is prohibited on Shabbos. When closing chametz closets or cupboards on Shabbos one may *wrap* string around the handles or use child-safety locks.]

☐ The *bitul chametz* formula usually recited when burning chametz must be recited before the end of the fifth hour. P. 160.

SEUDAH SHLISHIS:

☐ *Minchah* is scheduled earlier than usual in order to allow one to partake of *seudah shlishis* before the tenth hour. P. 151.

☐ Neither bread, matzah nor *matzah ashirah* are used at this meal. One may partake (depending on custom) of *kneidlach* (matzah balls), meat or fish, or fruits. [Sephardim with the custom to eat *matzah ashirah* on Pesach may use it for this meal before the tenth hour.] P. 164.

☐ After the tenth hour one may not partake of large satiating amounts of any food. Small amounts of fruit are permitted. P. 141.

MOTZAEI SHABBOS:

☐ No seder preparations may be made until after *tzeis hakochavim.* One must recite **Baruch HaMavdil bein Kodesh L'Kodesh** before beginning any Yom Tov preparations. P. 147.

TABLE OF TIMES

EREV PESACH – SHABBOS 5761 – APRIL 7, 2001

	A	B	C	D	E	F	G
Jerusalem, Israel	10:38	5:22	9:10	9:34	10:26	10:38	2:52
Baltimore, MD	11:04	6:17	9:36	10:00	10:52	11:04	3:23
Brooklyn, NY	10:54	6:08	9:25	9:49	10:42	10:54	3:13
Chicago, IL	10:47	6:04	9:18	9:42	10:35	10:47	3:08
Johannesburg, SA	11:12	5:43	9:49	10:13	11:00	11:12	3:05
London, England	10:56	6:24	9:25	9:49	10:44	10:56	3:23
Los Angeles, CA	10:51	6:00	9:23	9:47	10:31	10:51	3:07
Melbourne, AUS	11:25	5:48	10:04	10:28	11:13	11:25	3:14

EREV PESACH – SHABBOS 5765 – APRIL 23, 2005

	A	B	C	D	E	F	G
Jerusalem, Israel	10:32	5:33	9:02	9:26	10:20	10:32	2:56
Baltimore, MD	10:51	6:33	9:25	9:49	10:45	10:57	3:29
Brooklyn, NY	10:46	6:25	9:14	9:38	10:34	10:46	3:19
Chicago, IL	10:40	6:21	9:08	9:32	10:28	10:40	3:15
Johannesburg, SA	11:10	5:27	9:49	10:13	10:58	11:10	2:55
London, England	10:47	6:51	9:11	9:35	10:35	10:47	3:35
Los Angeles, CA	10:45	6:12	9:14	9:38	10:33	10:45	3:11
Melbourne, AUS	11:24	5:26	10:06	10:30	11:12	11:24	3:01

A. Preferred time for burning of chametz on Friday, according to the calculation of the *Gra*.

B. Candlelighting Friday, calculated at 18 minutes before sunset. Jerusalem is calculated at 40 minutes before sunset.

C. Latest time one is permitted to eat chametz on Shabbos according to the calculation of the *Magen Avraham*.*

D. Latest time one is permitted to eat chametz on Shabbos according to the calculation of the *Gra*.

E. Latest time for disposal of chametz on Shabbos according to the calculation of the *Magen Avraham*.*

F. Latest time for the disposal of chametz on Shabbos according to the calculation of the *Gra*.

G. The tenth hour (following the calculation of the *Gra*) before which time one must eat (the second) *Seudah Shlishis*.

NOTE: All times in the chart are standard time. One must ascertain that standard time is in fact being observed or make the proper adjustments.

* All calculations according to the *Magen Avraham* are based on the presumption that *alos hashachar* and *tzeis hakochavim* are seventy-two minutes before sunrise and after sunset respectively.